P9-DBO-734

TRUCS OF THE TRADE

TRUCS OF THE TRADE

101 Tricks, Tips, and Recipes from America's Greatest Chefs

Edited by Frank Ball and Arlene Feltman

Illustrations by Art Glazer

HarperPerennial
A Division of HarperCollins*Publishers*

FIRST EDITION

Designed by Charles Kreloff

Library of Congress Cataloging-in-Publication Data
Trucs of the trade: 101 tricks, tips, and recipes from America's greatest chefs / edited by Frank Ball and Arlene Feltman.
          p.   cm.
Includes index.
ISBN 0-06-096595-9
1. Cookery. I. Ball, Frank. II. Feltman, Arlene.
TX652.T786 1992
641.5—dc20   92-52622

92 93 94 95 96 ❖ / RRD 10 9 8 7 6 5 4 3 2 1

CONTENTS

INTRODUCTION

What is a *truc,* anyway?

And how do you say it?

It's easy to say, but it's a little harder to say what it is.

Let's start with the easy part. *Truc* is a French word. When it's pronounced it sounds like *true* with a *k* at the end: *true + k = TRUC.*

Now for the hard part.

Truc is, basically, "trick." Not a magic trick, based on illusion, but a trick in a bigger, more universal sense—a trick that offers the inherent satisfaction of beating reality, of finding a better, cheaper, easier, faster way of getting something done. A trick that, the mere knowing of which, makes you feel smug.

Trucs have particular relevance in the kitchen. Take potatoes, for instance. Potatoes have a natural, built-in tendency to get mushy and fall apart when they are boiled. But there's a trick—a better way—revealed here by Giuliano Bugialli, to keep potatoes intact. Every single time. That trick is a *truc.*

Sometimes a *truc* is a shortcut, a way of doing something faster—like chilling champagne in 20 minutes flat (*Truc #101*). That shortcut is a *truc.*

At times a *truc* is a gimmick—like cooking fish in paper, for instance (*Truc #76*), or tenderizing meat with wine corks (*Truc #66*). These gimmicks are definitely *trucs.*

At other times a *truc* is a tip, a special little procedure that delivers better results. Like the *truc* André Soltner uses to ensure that the omelets at Lutèce don't stick (*Truc #42*). Or the *truc* Anne Rosenzweig developed for creating the perfect hamburger (*Truc #63*). Or the *truc* master baker Jim Dodge uses to coax the pesky skin off hazelnuts (*Truc #89*).

Finally, a *truc* is sometimes an out-and-out secret. Like the way to cook perfect rice (*Truc #45*), gleefully revealed by Chef Patrick Clark who advises, "Begin by ignoring the directions on the box …"

Trucs are not created in the scholarly vacuum of a laboratory. Rather, they are discovered and developed in the heat of real-world kitchens, through the daily interaction between cooks and ingredients, implements and processes. Once discovered, *trucs* are shared and passed around from one cook to another, constituting a legacy, a treasure trove of professional knowledge.

No matter what their form or their source, though, all *trucs* share a single characteristic: a real *truc* is *genuinely helpful*. And that's the point.

We hope you enjoy learning these *trucs* and that you'll find them to be genuinely helpful. We are grateful to our many friends who shared their *trucs* with us, first for a videotape and now in this book. They were genuinely helpful. Their generosity reflects that of Kobrand Corporation, merchants of fine wines, who sponsored the production of the video.

In purchasing this book, you too have been genuinely helpful. A portion of the proceeds from this project—both video and book—goes to support the work of Share Our Strength (SOS), a network of food industry and other creative professionals united to fight hunger in the United States and overseas. Further information about the work of this organization and the video version of this book can be obtained by calling SOS at (800) 222-1767.

Thank you. And keep on *trucin'*.

F. B. & A. F.

THE TRUCS

VEGETABLES

#1
OPENING ARTICHOKES

When Mother Nature invented the packaging for artichokes, she created a doozie. Jimmy Schmidt *features artichokes so frequently on his menu that he had to find a fast, workable way to get to the heart of the matter. He developed this three-stroke* truc *for delivering the heart in four neat pieces.*

Quarter the cooked artichoke, lengthwise, cutting through the heart. Cut across each quarter, just at the point where the purple leaves peak. When the knife stops naturally, gently peel the heart and choke away from the tough leaves. Remove the fibrous choke from the heart by making a cut about ½ inch deep at the base of the choke fibers. Flick the blade of the knife up and the choke will pull right out, leaving the heart.

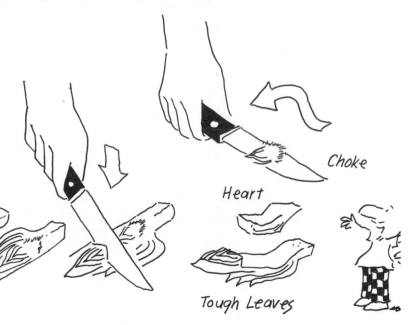

Choke

Heart

Tough Leaves

#2
PICTURE-PERFECT AVOCADOS

Picture-perfect avocado halves, deftly peeled to reveal their smooth green flesh, are lovely to behold. Their violin-like shape and their velvet texture coalesce to become a thing of beauty. Occasionally. More frequently the shape disappears and the texture is totally mutilated as we wrestle the peel off. Robert Del Grande says the truc *is in thinking small.*

Don't try to remove the peel in one piece. With the tip of a sharp paring knife, make two lengthwise slits, equally spaced, just through the skin of the avocado. Avoid cutting the flesh beneath. With the edge of the blade, lift the corner of the outside strip of skin and roll it off. Repeat with the other two strips.

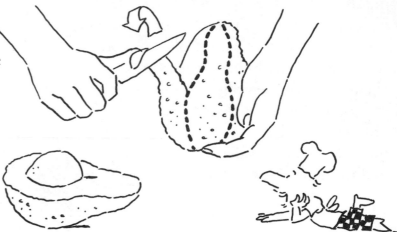

#3
PITTING AVOCADOS

When most of us North-of-the-border types try to open and pit an avocado, we end up with a handful of guacamole. Chef Robert Del Grande has an ingenious two-step truc that he gratefully learned from a Mexican colleague.

Start by trimming off the stem end of an unpeeled avocado. Then, hold the avocado on its side and work a knife around the seed, cutting it full circle. Remove the knife and give both sides of the avocado a gentle twist. The avocado will pull right apart into two halves. To remove the seed: hit the top of the seed with the heel of a heavy knife. Give the knife a slight turn and lift; the seed will emerge stuck to the blade.

To remove the seed from the knife, reach over the top of the blade with forefinger and thumb and push down, with a squeezing action, until the seed pops off.

#4
CONTROLLING THE TEXTURE OF DRIED BEANS

One of life's abiding mysteries: why do cooked dried beans sometimes come out mushy and creamy and, at other times, firm and whole. Is it due to the age of the beans, the preparation (soaking versus parboiling), the cooking liquid (broth versus water), the heat source (gas versus electric), the kind of pot (metal versus clay), or the size of the pot? Chef Judy Rogers *made a breakthrough discovery when she realized that the beans, the preparation, the liquid, the heat, and the pot are irrelevant factors; the* truc *to reliable bean cookery is in the lid.*

For soft and creamy beans, cook with the lid on.
For firmer beans, cook with the lid off.

Soft Beans   Firm Beans

#5
SNAPPING FAVA BEANS

Those strange, lumpy-looking oversized pods that show up in the market during the spring and summer are called fava beans. And they're good for you. They sport a rich, smooth taste that makes them a welcome accompaniment to meat, fish, and fowl. But many of us pass on favas for a simple reason: we don't know how to peel them. Daniel Boulud *to the rescue, with a* truc *that makes peeling favas a snap.*

Working down the pod, snap to release each fava bean and push it out with thumb and forefinger. Blanch the beans for 30 seconds in boiling water, then plunge them into iced water to cool. Break the seam of each bean with a fingernail, pushing the fava bean out of its sleeve.

#6
REMOVING BEET STAINS

Daniel Boulud has developed a defensive strategy against beet stains. When working with fresh beets, he covers himself and his work surface with a thin membrane of protection that ensures the stains end up in the trash and not on the cook or the kitchen.

Cover the work surface with wax paper and wear disposable rubber gloves when preparing fresh beets. At cleanup time, toss the gloves and the paper—and the stains.

#7
CARROTS THAT TASTE LIKE CARROTS

Carrots are a lot like tomatoes—they can be intensely flavorful or they can be intensely tasteless. Giuliano Bugialli, *observing that a great deal of the carrot's flavor resides in the carrot's skin, uses that skin to intensify the sweet, "carroty" flavor of boiled carrots. His* truc:

Don't peel the carrots. Wash them and cook with the peels on, in salted boiling water. Once they are soft enough to pierce with a fork, plunge them into cool water. The peels will rub right off, leaving behind their distinctive flavor.

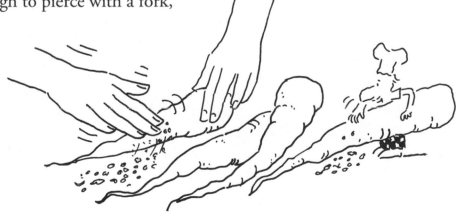

#8
ODORLESS CAULIFLOWER COOKING

Among the special pleasures of home-cooked food is the delightful smell that emanates from the kitchen. Unless it's cauliflower. Then everyone wants to eat out. For as good as cauliflower can taste on the plate, it can really smell up a house while it's cooking. Antoine Bouterin's truc, which also works with broccoli and cabbage, is like a breath of fresh air.

Tear a slice of bread into small pieces and add it to the pot with the cauliflower and its cooking liquid. The bread will absorb and contain the cooking odor.

#9
CUTTING CUCUMBER FANS WITH CHOPSTICKS

————

One of Barbara Tropp's most popular dishes is Ma-La Szechwan Cucumber Fans—marinated pieces of cucumber cleverly cut and splayed to resemble fans. Chef Tropp reveals her chopstick trick for making these fanciful fans (and points out that the same approach will work with zucchini, carrots, potatoes, and so forth).

Place two chopsticks flat on the counter and bring the thicker ends together to form a *V*. Put a 2- to 3-inch piece of peeled cucumber on the counter, in between the chopsticks. Cut the cucumber into thin slices. (The chopsticks will automatically stop the knife from cutting through the cucumber.) Apply light pressure on the vegetable to spread open the slices and reveal the fan shape.

#10
EGGPLANT GENDER

Male or female, which is sweeter? If we're talking people, the jury's still out. But if we're talking eggplant, the males win hands down—they've got fewer bitter seeds. So to end up with better eggplant dishes, start out with male eggplants. Granted, a good male is hard to find, but Lidia Bastianich *knows how ... and she's telling.*

To determine the gender of eggplants, look at the bottom of the vegetable where the flower was once attached. The male eggplant has a well-rounded bottom with a smooth, even stem area. The female has a narrow bottom with an elliptical, deeply indented stem area.

Male

Female

#11
A SMASHING WAY TO PEEL GARLIC

Removing the peel from garlic is sufficiently frustrating to make even a patient cook want to smash it. And that, according to our friend the late Leslee Reis, *is exactly what should be done.*

Place the head of garlic on the counter and press on the root end to loosen the cloves. Separate a clove from the head and set it on a cutting board. Lay the flat side of a chef's knife on the clove and press down firmly until the clove snaps. Pick up the clove and the peel will come right off.

#12
MELLOWING GARLIC

The lusty, robust taste of garlic is just right for most people. But for those who want their garlic slightly less lusty and a little less robust, Michel Richard *discloses this Gallic* truc *for mellowing the taste of garlic.*

Peel the skin from a clove of garlic. Using a sharp paring knife, make a vertical incision halfway into the clove, removing the bitter green shoot, if present, from the center. Put the clove in a pot of water and boil for 5 minutes.

#13
MINCING GARLIC WITH A FORK

When making a vinaigrette or other salad dressing that calls for minced garlic, using a garlic press or a cutting board to mince the garlic just creates more things to wash. Alain Sailhac shares an ingenious little truc he learned from his father—a way to mince the garlic using just the bowl and fork used to make the dressing.

Place a fork, tines pointing up, on the bottom of the salad bowl. Gently rub a peeled garlic clove across the ends of the tines, mincing the garlic. When garlic is minced, add remaining ingredients and proceed with the recipe.

#14
NO-FUSS GARLIC PURÉE

Puréeing garlic in a garlic press couldn't be easier. Cleaning a garlic press couldn't be harder. So Susan Feniger uses her garlic press as seldom as possible. Instead, when she needs to purée garlic, she resorts to this truc.

Cut a garlic clove in half lengthwise and place it flat-side down on a work surface. Make several vertical cuts, then several horizontal cuts on each half of the clove. Finish by cutting straight down across the clove, mincing the garlic. Sprinkle the garlic with a little salt and, using the flat side of a chef's knife, mash the garlic and salt together. The abrasiveness of the salt helps turn the garlic into a smooth purée.

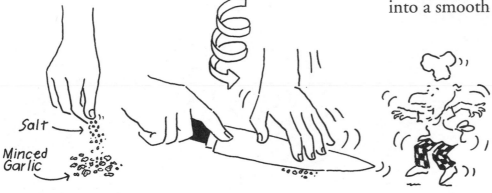

Salt →

Minced Garlic →

#15
GETTING THE GARLIC ON THE BREAD

In Italy, garlic bread is called bruschetta. *The concept is simple: slices of hearty peasant bread are toasted, rubbed with garlic, and topped simply with tomatoes, mushrooms, and/or olive oil. There's one special trick involved in this process: how do you get the garlic rubbed on the bread without mangling and tearing the bread's crisp, toasted surface? Native Tuscan* Pino Luongo *imparts this native Tuscan* truc.

Rub a clove of garlic liberally *on just the crusty edges* around the perimeter of the toasted bread. The rough texture of the crust grates the garlic and flavors the whole slice.

#16
TEARLESS ONION DICING

Susan Feniger has been working on a truc *to make all existing onions practically no-tear. She's discovered that by dicing an onion in a way that minimizes the loss of its juices, the onion has better flavor, caramelizes evenly when cooking—and, most important, doesn't cause tears. Here's how it's done.*

Minimize the release of the onion's tear-causing juice by cutting the onion cleanly, precisely, and as few times as possible. Set the onion on its root end and cut it in half, right through the core. Place a half, flat-side down on the cutting board and make several lengthwise cuts, then several crosswise. Dice finely by cutting straight down through the onion.

1. Vertical Cuts

3. Cut Straight Down

2. Horizontal Cuts

#17
KEEPING THE SWEETNESS IN RAW ONION

Ever notice how raw onion gets stronger as it sits? How a bowl of potato salad with onion becomes, after a few hours, a bowl of onion salad? How a sprightly fresh tomato/onion salsa turns on you to become salsa from hell? Well, there's a reason: chemicals within onions are released when an onion is cut. These chemicals oxidize as they sit, becoming increasingly strong, bitter, and unpleasant. The solution? A simple chemical truc from Mr. Wizard, Rick Bayless.

Place diced or chopped onion in a strainer. Dip the strainer several times into a bowl filled with water and and a little bit of vinegar. Drain the onion, shaking off excess liquid. The acid in the water prevents the onion from turning bitter.

#18
BETTER SCALLION CHOPPING

Finely chopping scallions isn't as easy as it might seem. Cutting across the white part reveals a series of concentric rings which, if they separate, is great; if they don't: scallion chunks result. And cutting across the green part frequently produces something akin to grade school paper dolls—a string of semi-detached scallion rings which appear to be holding hands. Barbara Tropp contributes a most helpful *truc* to achieve perfectly chopped scallions.

Before cutting a scallion crosswise, make one vertical slice all the way from the root to the tip. This one extra cut will allow the rings to separate easily and will double the number of scallion pieces produced.

#19
PEELING PEPPERS QUICKLY

One of the few vegetables that a vegetable peeler won't peel is a fresh pepper. The peel is so thin and so tightly bound to the flesh that it takes heat to get it off. The usual method is to blacken the skin over an open flame (impossible with an electric range) or under the broiler. The pepper has to be repeatedly turned to expose different areas to the flames, and even then, there are nooks and crannies that escape. This inefficient process takes several minutes and it is incredibly boring. Zarela Martinez has a truc that takes the pepper from the fire into the frying pan—and polishes off the job in less than 30 seconds.

Pour vegetable oil into a skillet to a depth of approximately ½ inch; heat until almost smoking. Make a small slit in the side of the pepper to prevent it from popping. Put the pepper into the skillet of hot oil and cook for a few seconds until the pepper turns beige in color and the skin becomes transparent. Turn and repeat on the other side. Remove the pepper, cool on a paper towel, and slip off the peel under running water.

#20
CUTTING PEPPERS FROM THE INSIDE OUT

The slick, waxy skin on bell peppers makes them a potential hazard on the cutting board— it's all too easy for a knife blade to slip when confronting this kind of surface. So Chef Michael Foley *turns things around with an inside-out truc for safely cutting bell peppers.*

After the pepper is seeded and deveined, place it on a cutting board *shiny side down*. Proceed to cut through the moist underside. The knife cuts easily through this surface and is less likely to slip.

#21
INSTANT GLOVES

Everybody knows that the skin and seeds of chili peppers contain hot resins that will burn a cook's hands. And everybody's been told endlessly to wear rubber gloves when working with chilies. And everybody usually ignores this advice because it's too much trouble to find the rubber gloves and put them on, particularly when working with just a few chilies. And everybody's been burned. And, therefore, everybody will love Stephan Pyles's truc for instant gloves.

To don instant gloves, rub the hands liberally with vegetable oil. This coating will protect the skin from the fiery resins in chili peppers.

#22
CLEANING DRIED CHILIES

Dean Fearing, *one of the guiding lights in Southwestern cuisine, illuminates for us a three-step* truc *for cleaning dried chilies quickly.*

To clean a dried chili, start by removing its stem. Then pull the chili apart, lengthwise, splitting it in half. Brush the seeds from both halves and the chili is ready to cook.

#23
QUICK PEPPER SEEDING

Most recipes which use fresh peppers specify that they be seeded. (In the case of sweet bell peppers and other mild varieties, the seeds have no taste and are extraneous; in the case of chili peppers, the seeds contain heat that overpowers the taste of the pepper.) Cutting the pepper in half and trying to dig out the seeds makes one feel like a strip miner or a dentist. The pros go about it a whole different way, a secret shared by Robert Del Grande.

Cut both ends off the pepper. Stand the pepper on the counter and slice straight down with a sharp knife, removing the flesh in four or five pieces from around the core. Discard the seeds and the core.

Cut   Cut

#24
KEEPING BOILED POTATOES FIRM

Sliced or cubed, potatoes boiled for salad need to be cooked until they're tender, but still retain their shape. Giuliano Bugialli shares a secret-ingredient truc he uses to keep the boiled potatoes from becoming mushy and falling apart.

Fill a pot with 2 parts water and 1 part vinegar. Add a dash of kosher salt and bring to a boil. Add the potatoes, which are already trimmed or peeled, and gently boil them until cooked.

#25
BAKING POTATOES ON COPPER PIPES

David Burke is known to be highly inventive in his novel combination of ingredients. And in the case of one of his signature garnishes, a crispy arched potato wafer, his inventiveness led him to devise a new kind of copper cookware—pipes.

Place a 2-inch-wide copper pipe (available at plumbing and building supply stores) on a baking sheet, using crumpled aluminum foil under the ends to keep the pipe from rolling. Preheat the pipe for 10 minutes in a 325° oven.

Thinly slice a peeled potato on a mandolin. Soak the slices in either flavored oil or clarified butter. Lay the slices across the pipe and bake in a 325° oven for 5 to 7 minutes. Once baked, the crispy wafers will easily slide off the pipe and retain their arched shape.

#26
EASY TOMATO PEELING

Peeling tomatoes with a knife is not only tedious and wasteful, but it yields a tomato that looks slightly brutalized. There's a better way. Andy D'Amico's truc makes peeling fast and easy, and delivers tomatoes with smooth, unnicked flesh. (This same approach, by the way, works well with peaches.)

Cut the core from the center of the tomato. Turn it over and score the bottom with a shallow *X*. Drop the tomato into boiling water, letting it simmer for about 10 seconds. With a slotted spoon, scoop up the tomato and plunge it into iced water. After cooling 30 seconds, the skin will slip right off.

#27
CUBING TOMATOES

Recipes frequently ask for tomatoes that are "peeled, seeded, and chopped." Peeling is easy (see Truc #26). But seeded and chopped is a little more daunting. If we cut the tomato in half and squeeze it to get the seeds out, we've effectively crushed it and cut it into a shape that's difficult to chop. If we section it and chop it first, we end up with several dozen nicely chopped pieces—all containing seeds. Paula Wolfert has come up with a new approach that solves these problems and delivers neat square shapes from round tomatoes. Paula calls this "cubing."

To cube a peeled tomato, begin by cutting across the tomato, about 1 inch down from the top, until the blade reaches the far side. Turning the knife blade, continue the cut down the side of the tomato. This creates a long strip of tomato; set that strip aside. Continue cutting around and down the tomato removing the flesh in a series of petals, using the natural contour of the tomato as a guide while cutting down its sides. With the tip of a finger, flick out any seeds that are attached to the petals and any remaining in the central core. The tomato is now peeled and seeded, ready to chop into neat squares, large or small as the recipe requires.

#28
A QUICK WAY TO CRUSH TOMATOES

Professional chefs use their hands in a variety of clever ways that don't normally occur to amateurs. Pino Luongo shares his truc for a "handy" tomato crusher.

Open a can of whole tomatoes, drain if desired, and pour the tomatoes into a large bowl. With one hand squeeze and crush them into either a rough or smooth consistency as required by the recipe.

#29
ROASTING TOMATOES

Modern tomatoes need all the help they can get. Rick Bayless *reports that roasting is a kind of culinary shock treatment that makes ordinary tomatoes good, and good tomatoes extraordinary. "High heat so concentrates and enhances the flavor," says Rick, "that the tomatoes acquire an entirely new taste dimension, perfect for soups and sauces." Roasting tomatoes couldn't be easier:*

Place a single layer of tomatoes on a foil-lined baking sheet, making sure the tomatoes don't touch. Place under a preheated broiler, several inches below the element, and roast for 10 to 15 minutes, turning them once. When the tomatoes blister and blacken on all sides, remove them from the oven. When cool enough to handle, slip off the peels.

#30
SAVING LEFTOVER TOMATO PASTE

Many recipes calls for tomato paste. More accurately, many recipes call for 1 tablespoon of tomato paste. What, then, does one do with the rest of the can? The late Leslee Reis shared with us her resourceful truc for saving tomato paste.

Measure leftover tomato paste by the tablespoon into individual compartments of an ice cube tray. Freeze, then pop the frozen spoonfuls of tomato paste into a zipper-seal bag and hold in the freezer for future use.

FRUITS

#31
"EFFICIENT" JUICING

Getting more for less is the height of efficiency. Stephan Pyles squeezes out a particularly efficient truc that helps him get the most juice out of a citrus fruit with the least amount of effort.

Pressing down on the fruit, roll it several times back and forth over a hard surface before cutting it in half. Squeezing the juice out will be effortless.

#32
PEELING AND SEGMENTING CITRUS FRUITS

Individual peeled segments of lemon, lime, orange, or grapefruit are a wonderful garnish. Patrick Clark *has a* truc *for preparing whole, membrane- and pith-free segments.*

The secret is in the approach: first cut off both ends of the fruit with a sharp paring knife and set the fruit flat on a work surface. Work the knife down along the natural rounded shape of the fruit, cutting off both the bitter pith and peel. Then hold the peeled fruit and slice down between the membranes to free each segment.

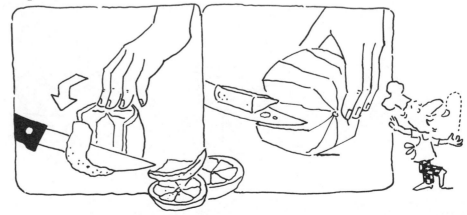

#33
BROAD-STROKE ZESTING

Many recipes call for the grated zest of citrus, the colored part of the peel that contains the fragrant oil. Most often a hand grater is used, a choice that yields tiny gratings. But Robert Del Grande goes about it differently. He removes the zest in large pieces, expanding the options for how it can be shaped and used— minced, chopped, or julienned.

Use a vegetable peeler to scrape a ribbon of peel off the fruit. Remove only the colored peel, leaving the bitter white pith attached to the fruit. Finish the peel by mincing, chopping, or julienning as desired.

Minced   Julienned

#34
GRATING CITRUS PEEL A BETTER WAY

Removing the tiny bits of grated peel from a grater can be the toughest part of adding citrus zest, or peel, to a recipe. Giuliano Bugialli has a special truc *for removing these stubborn bits from the grater with a paper-thin layer of … paper!*

Cover the side of a grater with a piece of parchment paper. Rub the citrus fruit back and forth, turning the fruit as the peel is scraped off. Lift the parchment paper off the grater. The grated peel remains on the paper and can be easily scraped into a bowl. The bitter white pith is left behind on the grater and can be simply washed away.

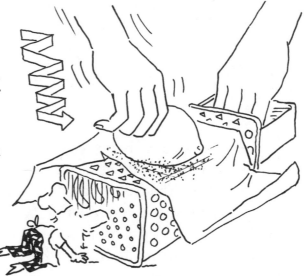

#35
DRY-POACHING PEARS IN SALT

___

Pears are well suited to poaching in either sugar, syrup, or wine. But there's one drawback—the poaching liquid dilutes somewhat the delicate taste of the pear. So Jimmy Schmidt dry-poaches his pears with a truc that sears in the pear's juices, trapping them beneath the peel. The key to successful dry-poaching is baking the salt until it is extremely hot, otherwise a salty taste will permeate through the peel. Cooked properly, the fruit will have no taste of salt and will be delicious served with a wine sauce or ice cream—or both.

Preheat a deep baking pan filled with kosher salt to 450° for 60 minutes. Insert a wooden skewer into the top of the fruit. Bury the fruit in the hot salt, leaving only a portion of the wooden skewer exposed. Bake for 15 minutes or until the fruit softens. Remove the fruit and brush off any clinging salt. Cool before serving.

#36
PORCUPINE-CUT MANGO

Craig Claiborne *visited Bali and came home with a neat* truc *that seems to be the right way to cut and serve a mango. In Bali, this presentation is dressed with a lime wedge.*

Hold the mango on end and slice the fruit in half, cutting down alongside the flat side of the broad seed. Take a mango half and score the flesh diagonally, making diagonal cuts every ¾ inch. Be careful not to cut through the rind. Give the fruit a quarter turn and continue scoring the flesh, cutting it into a diamond-shaped pattern. Pick up the fruit and, using thumbs, push the skin up, pressing the fruit outward, as if turning a tennis ball inside out. The flesh opens to reveal little porcupine-like spikes of mango, which can easily be lifted from the peel with the edge of a spoon.

#37
SEEDING A POMEGRANATE NEATLY

Paula Wolfert *makes great use of pomegranates. She sprinkles the seeds on salads, adds them to stuffings, and squeezes them and uses the juice for tenderizing marinades. This versatile fruit has only one drawback—the seeds stain like crazy. The trick is knowing how to open a pomegranate and remove the seeds so they don't stain everything in sight. Here's how Paula liberates those seeds—her "stainless steal"* truc.

Make a slit in the center of the fruit, large enough to insert both your thumbs. Submerge the fruit in a bowl of water. Insert your thumbs in the slit and pull the fruit apart into two pieces. Loosen the seeds with your fingers; they will float to the surface, rinsed and ready to be scooped out and used.

EGGS

#38
TELLING A BOILED EGG FROM A RAW ONE

Raw eggs and hard-boiled eggs are radically different on the inside, but from the outside they look alike. How does one, from the outside, manage to tell what's going on inside? Chef Hubert Keller's truc reveals the egg's status with a simple twist of the wrist.

To determine whether an egg is raw or hard-boiled, give it a spin. A hard-boiled egg will spin easily; a raw egg won't spin at all.

Cooked   Raw

#39
COOKING THE "PERFECT" HARD-BOILED EGG

Many people have a litany of troubles concerning their hard-boiled eggs: the eggs crack while cooking, they're undercooked, they have a sinister gray rim around the yolk, or they stick to the shell and won't peel. André Soltner imparts a three-step truc *that solves all the problems.*

Start with eggs that are at least one day old and are at room temperature. In a pot large enough to hold the eggs in a single layer, bring cold water to a boil. When the water is boiling, not before, place the eggs in the pot. Boil 8 minutes for small eggs; 10 minutes for large ones. Remove eggs from heat and cool immediately in several changes of cold water.

Boil 8 to 10 Minutes.

#40
HARD-BOILED EGG GARNISH

The hard-cooked egg is a universal plate decoration, usually presented in familiar slices or wedges. Daniel Boulud has a truc that elevates the ordinary hard-boiled egg into a delicate, elegant garnish, classically known as mimosa.

Separate the white from the yolk. Rub the egg white through one side of a fine-mesh sieve, set aside. Then rub the yolk through other side of the sieve. Sprinkle the white and yolk in alternating circles to create an attractive garnish.

#41
OPENING QUAIL EGGS

Quail eggs are turning up on lots of menus, usually presented poached or fried where their diminutive size is shown to best advantage. The problem is that quail eggs are really tiny (about the size of a thumbnail) and fragile—and are, therefore, tricky to open. How do those in the know manage to crack and open the shell without smashing the egg inside? Jean-Louis Palladin *reveals the best, and probably the* only, *way to open a quail egg.*

Notice that a quail egg has both a pointed end and flat end. Working at the flat end, take a small paring knife and gently press the tip of the blade into the shell, cracking the shell while turning the egg. Make a continuous circle around the egg, lift off the top, and carefully pour out the egg.

#42
KEY TO A PERFECT OMELET

"In France, when a young chef shows up at a restaurant looking for work, they ask him to make an omelet," remembers André Soltner. *"And properly so. There's so much technique involved that if a chef makes a perfect omelet—you know, you just know, that chef's been well trained."* Is there a truc? *Definitely.* *"If your pan isn't clean, you'll never have a good omelet because your eggs will stick,"* says André. Here's his truc *for getting the pan spotlessly clean.*

Pour some kosher salt into the skillet and rub vigorously with a kitchen towel over the side and bottom of the pan. The abrasiveness of the salt will put a fine polish on the skillet. Discard the salt and proceed with the recipe.

GRAINS

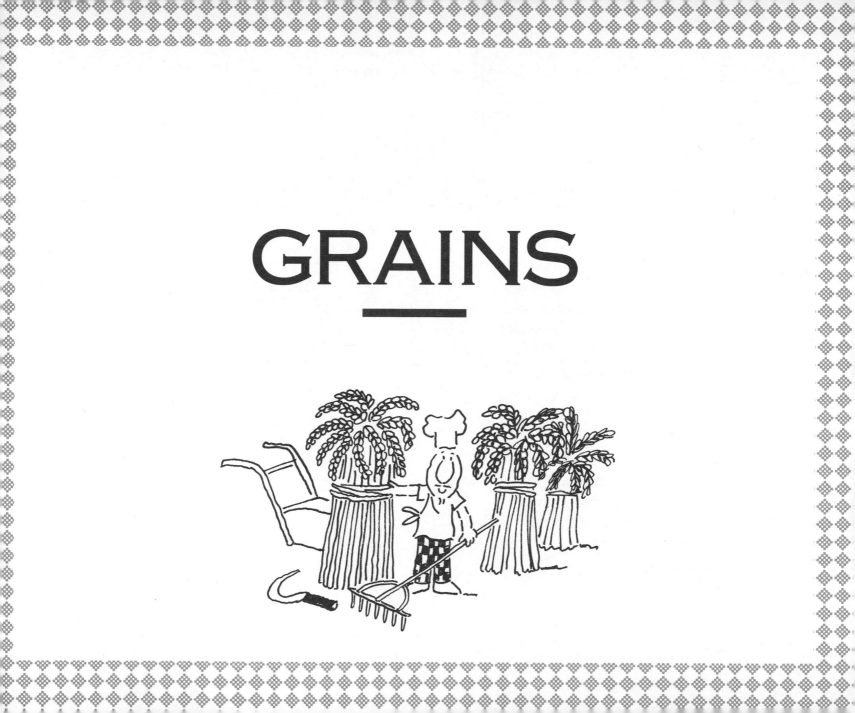

#43
QUICK BRICK OVEN TRICK

The disappointing results which most home bakers face when they try to create hearty thick-crusted peasant bread or thin-crisp pizza crust has very little to do with ingredients and proportions; it has a lot to do with having the wrong kind of oven. A brick oven contributes uniquely and unmistakably to the texture and taste of these breads. Giuliano Bugialli has a quick brick trick for obtaining these results from any oven.

Place a single layer of large unglazed terra cotta tiles (available from a brickyard, masonry supply, or tile store) on an oven rack. Preheat the oven. Then place the bread or pizza directly on the tiles and bake.

#44
MAKING LUMP-FREE POLENTA

"I've been eating polenta ever since I was a kid—and cooking it since I was big enough to reach the pot," says Lidia Bastianich. *"About the only way it should not be served is with lumps."* She accomplishes lump-free polenta with this truc *she learned from her grandmother.*

The secret of lump-free polenta is starting with cold water. Mix the cornmeal thoroughly with the cold water, then season with salt and a bay leaf, and cook. Many recipes specify warm or hot water, but lump-free polenta starts with cold water.

Cold Water

#45
MAKING PERFECT RICE EVERY TIME

"The secret to turning out perfectly cooked rice," according to Patrick Clark, *"lies in completely ignoring the directions on the back of the box."* Patrick's truc *for preparing perfectly cooked rice couldn't be easier.*

In a saucepan over medium heat, sauté the rice in a little oil until the kernels are well coated.

Rice   Oil   Water

Add an amount of water equal to the amount of rice (1 cup to 1 cup, for example). Bring the water to a boil, stir, and then reduce the heat to a simmer. Cover and cook the rice for 10 minutes. Remove the pan from the heat and, with the lid still on, let it sit for 15 minutes. Fluff the rice with a fork.

#46
SALVAGING BURNED RICE

That ancient Chinese New Year's greeting, "May your rice never burn," tells us that this is not a new problem. The late Felipe Rojas-Lombardi *had a new* truc *for solving this old problem, a way of actually salvaging scorched rice with … onion skins.*

To remove the smoky, unpleasant taste from scorched rice, scoop the rice into a clean pot, being careful *not* to scrape in any of the crusty bottom at the same time. Place a single layer of onion skins on top of the rice. Cover the pot and let it sit for 10 to 15 minutes. The onion skins will remove the acrid taste from the rice. Discard the onion skins and serve.

#47
MEASURING RICE FOR RISOTTO

To make risotto, that creamy, rich Italian specialty made with short-grain Arborio rice, an unspecified quantity of liquid is added to an unspecified quantity of rice and cooked for an unspecified period of time—"until the rice is soft and will absorb no more liquid." So how much rice to start with? Pino Luongo's truc *offers a good rule of thumb for figuring this out.*

For risotto, use *one handful* of raw Arborio rice for each person being served.

#48
ARTICHOKE-FLAVORED RICE

Rice is often served as an edible sponge for gravy or sauce. With some plain, unsauced entrées, plain boiled rice would be the perfect accompaniment—if only it had some flavor. The late Felipe Rojas-Lombardi unveiled a secret that gives boiled rice a haunting, elusive, intriguing flavor—and makes it good enough to stand unclothed.

Cut a whole raw artichoke into quarters. Place one or more quarters of the artichoke in the pot along with the rice and water and cook as usual. Remove the artichoke before serving.

#49
SOFTENING TORTILLAS IN A MICROWAVE OVEN

Rolling up ingredients inside a corn tortilla is fundamental in Mexican cooking. Such popular dishes as enchiladas, taquitos, *and* flautas *capitalize on the appeal of this edible envelope. But rolling commercially made tortillas is not easy because they tend to be dry and brittle and, therefore, tend to crack and split as they're rolled.* Zarela Martinez *developed a speedy* truc *for making corn tortillas soft, pliable, and easy to roll.*

Place several tortillas into a plastic bag and loosely close the bag. Microwave on high for 30 seconds. The tortillas will emerge soft and pliable enough to roll easily, without breaking.

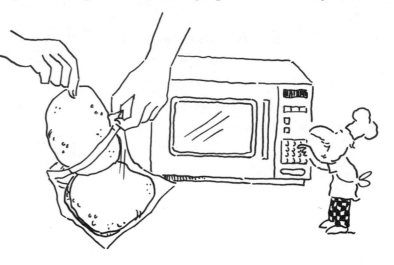

HERBS AND SPICES

#50
PRESERVING FRESH HERBS

When herbs are fresh and abundant, Lidia Bastianich *preserves her favorites in an elegantly simple manner—she freezes them. Then for the rest of year, Lidia has a plentiful supply of fragrant herbs.*

To preserve fresh herbs, pick the unbruised leaves from their stems and splash them with cold water. Pack several tablespoonfuls into small paper cups, fill the cup with water, and freeze. To use, defrost under running water and proceed as with fresh herbs.

#51
KEEPING FRESH CILANTRO FRESH

Fresh cilantro is an essential ingredient in much Mexican and Asian cooking. Since there's no substitute for it, it's the kind of ingredient that's good to have on hand. But keeping cilantro fresh for more than a day is a real challenge. The leaves begin to bruise and turn black very quickly. Andy D'Amico has discovered a truc for keeping cilantro fresh, green, and usable for several days.

Pick the leaves off the stem and place them in a single layer on a moist paper towel. Roll up the towel, and wrap it tightly in plastic wrap or seal it in a zipper-seal plastic bag, squeezing out the excess air. Refrigerate; the cilantro will stay green and fresh for several days.

#52
REFRESHING WHOLE SPICES

—

Peppercorns, juniper berries, and other whole spices lose some of their pungency after being packaged for a long time. Andrew D'Amico has a truc for refreshing tired spices and restoring their punch.

Roast dried whole spices in a preheated 350° oven for a few minutes. When the spices become aromatic, remove them from the oven and grind or use whole as the recipe requires.

#53
PRESERVING FRESH BASIL IN OIL

"Oh, I love the smell of sweet basil!" enthuses Michel Richard. *To use that flavor all year long, Michel has a wonderful* truc *for keeping the basil fragrant and fresh. But wait, there's more. This* truc *yields a bonus—basil-flavored oil that's perfect to use in risottos, pastas, vinaigrettes, and* bruschetta.

Pick off the unbruised basil leaves from the stem. Pack the leaves in a jar and then cover completely with olive oil. Close the lid tightly and refrigerate.

#54
USING FRESH HERB STEMS

The late Felipe Rojas-Lombardi *used fresh herbs extensively in his cooking. He used the leaves, of course, for finishing dishes and for garnish—but he also used the stems. He reminded us that "the flavor of the herb is in the stem as well as the leaves," and then disclosed an economical* truc *for using the stems.*

Use the stems of fresh herbs in preparing soups, stocks, and long-simmered sauces. The stems will deliver flavor just like the leaves, and because they have less chlorophyll, they will not tint the product green.

#55
CUTTING FRESH HERBS

Most of us have trouble turning out precise, fine cuts of the larger herb leaves, such as basil and sorrel; we usually end up with a pile of hacked, bruised leaves of wildly different shapes and sizes. There is a better way. Larry Forgione *lets us in on the secret.*

Remove fresh herb leaves from the stems and stack them. Roll the leaves lengthwise tightly. With a small knife, cut across the rolled bundle of leaves in thin strips. This creates long, thin julienned slices of herb. For finely minced herbs, turn the julienned slices (still rolled) 45° and cut crosswise into very thin strips.

Unroll For Julienne

Cut Crosswise To Mince

#56
HEALTHY HERBS

Chef David Bouley *has discovered yet another benefit of vitamin C—it keeps fresh herbal oils from turning brown. Here's his prescription.*

For each 6 ounces of oil, use one 500-milligram tablet of vitamin C. Crush the vitamin tablet and combine it with the oil in a blender; blend until dissolved. Add fresh green herb leaves and blend until they are completely puréed. Refrigerated, this oil will keep its green color indefinitely.

SAUCES, BROTHS, AND DRESSINGS

#57
INTENSE FISH STOCK

Fish stock is the foundation on which memorable fish chowders, soups, stews, and countless other fish dishes are built. The most important requirement of fish stock is that it be intensely fishy. Most cooks know that cooking down a meat stock intensifies its flavor; the same technique does not work for fish stock. Jasper White *shares the surprisingly obvious* truc *behind intense fish stock.*

Intense fish stock depends on fish, not cooking time. Fish stock cooked more than 20 minutes will begin to turn bitter. The only way to intensify fish stock is to start with a larger quantity of fish parts.

Only 20 Minutes!

#58
MAKING A LIGHTER VINAIGRETTE

Sometimes traditional vinaigrette formulations seem too heavy in weight and overpowering in taste for dressing tender, delicate salad green suchs as Boston lettuce or mâche. Jean-Georges Vongerichten *divulges a* truc *that'll lighten even the heaviest vinaigrette.*

When making vinaigrette, either by hand or in a food processor, add a couple of teaspoons of boiling water after the dressing emulsifies.

Boiling Water

#59
MAKING PERFECT WINE SAUCE

A well-made wine sauce is smooth tasting, redolent with the flavor of the wine, but bearing no harsh acidic edge. There's a truc *to pulling that off. The trick is in preparing the wine before it's incorporated into the sauce.* Georges Perrier, *renowned for his classic technique, shares the secret.*

Bring the wine to a boil, then ignite it with a match. The flame will burn off the wine's alcohol and acidity at the same time. Then bring back the wine's sweetness by adding just a touch of sugar. This mixture is now ready to incorporate into the sauce.

#60
HOW NOT TO SPOIL THE BROTH

Contrary to popular wisdom, it's not too many cooks that spoil the broth, it's bacteria. During the cooling-down period—after the stock is cooked and before it's refrigerated—bacteria can begin to form, multiply, and sour the stock. Marcel Desaulniers shares his truc *for quickly getting stock cooled down and ready for the refrigerator.*

To cool a soup or stock as quickly as possible, place the pot into an ice bath, one that reaches midway up the stock's container. Stir the stock often, and it will cool quickly. Once the stock is cool to the touch, refrigerate immediately.

#61
REPAIRING A TOO-SALTY SAUCE

Adding salt to a sauce is easy. Removing salt from a sauce is a little tricky. Fortunately, Antoine Bouterin *has a little* truc.

Dip a sugar cube into the too-salty sauce and pass it back and forth in a zigzag motion across the surface of the sauce. Repeat three or four times. Taste and repeat if necessary.

#62
FIXING "BROKEN" MAYONNAISE

Homemade mayonnaise, that delightful blend of egg yolks, oil, and seasonings, is a special pleasure, better by far than store-bought. But homemade mayo has an undeserved reputation for being "difficult." Many a cook's had a nice batch of mayonnaise suddenly "break" and lose its texture, turning thin and soupy. André Soltner has a wonderfully simple truc *for rebinding broken mayonnaise, whatever the cause.*

When mayonnaise breaks, take a clean bowl and add a couple of spoons of warm (not boiling) water. Very slowly pour the broken mayonnaise into the second bowl, whisking to incorporate the water. The mayonnaise will re-emulsify, thicken up … and be "fixed."

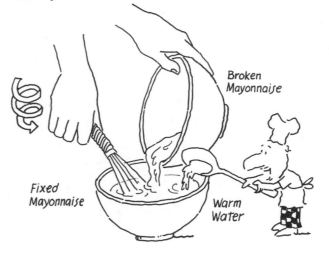

Broken Mayonnaise

Fixed Mayonnaise

Warm Water

MEATS AND POULTRY

#63
MAKING THE PERFECT HAMBURGER

——

Grilling a hamburger patty presents a culinary challenge: how to cook it fast enough and hot enough so it'll be seared and browned on the outside, yet remain rare and juicy on the inside. Anne Rosenzweig *engineered the solution: pack something cold and flavorable in the middle of the patty. This is the* truc *behind (inside?) her famous burger.*

Before grilling, tuck a tablespoon-size nugget of frozen herb butter (parsley and shallots is a good combination) into the center of a freshly ground hamburger patty. This nugget keeps the hamburger rare in the center, while giving it an extra burst of flavor.

#64
UNNATURAL SAUSAGE CASING

The toughest part to making homemade link sausages is locating a source for the natural casings. In many parts of the country they're almost impossible to find. But Michel Richard *has discovered an easy substitute for natural casing, universally available in every supermarket in the land.*

Prepare the filling for your favorite sausage. Lay a piece of plastic wrap flat on a counter and place the sausage filling along the near edge. Fold the plastic wrap over the filling and press the wrap tightly against it, making it as tight as possible. Roll the sausage into a log shape, keeping the roll tight. Twist the endstogether and tie them off with a knot. Simmer this sausage in broth or water until it is cooked.

Once cooked, rewrap the sausages and refrigerate. To brown the sausages, remove wrapping and sauté before serving.

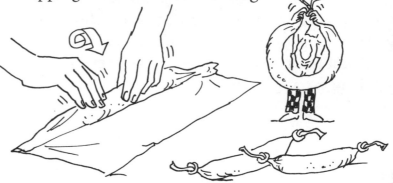

#65
SELF-BASTING BIRDS

Everyone knows that frequent basting helps ensure a beautifully browned, succulent roasted chicken. Michael Roberts has a truc *for achieving that same result without the need for frequent basting. A real time-saver, Michael's* truc *also works with capons, turkeys, and other birds, either stuffed or unstuffed.*

Season and prepare the chicken for roasting. Before placing the bird in the oven, lay a piece of cheesecloth saturated with olive oil or melted chicken fat over the bird so that the bird's completely covered. Roast as usual. Then, once cooked, remove the cheesecloth to reveal a golden brown, moist bird.

Olive Oil Or Chicken Fat

Cheesecoth

#66
TENDERIZING MEAT WITH WINE CORKS

Long-cooked, slow-simmered stews may be the ultimate comfort food. The only problem is that, by definition, the cooking process is long and slow. The late Felipe Rojas-Lombardi *uncorked a* truc *that delivers that long-cooked, slow-simmered taste faster.*

When making a stew, add at least three wine corks to the pot. These corks release enzymes that help tenderize the meat quickly and reduce the cooking time by as much as half. Remember to remove the corks before serving.

#67
SEVEN-MINUTE
"ROASTED" CHICKEN

Preparing oven-roasted chicken with its characteristic crispy skin and moist, juicy flesh takes well over an hour. But Anne Rosenzweig has developed an ingenious truc for putting this culinary staple on the table in about 7 minutes!

Bone a 3½-pound chicken, keeping the breast and thigh meat in one piece. (Reserve remainder of chicken for another use.) Season with salt and pepper. Heat 1 tablespoon of oil medium-high in a skillet. When hot, add the chicken, skin side down, and cook until the skin gets very crispy, about 2 minutes. Place the pan in a preheated 400° oven for approximately 5 minutes until the chicken is done.

FISH AND SEAFOOD

#68
A COOL WAY TO OPEN CLAMS

Intimidated about opening clams? Lidia Bastianich *has some advice. "Relax. Both you and the clams." It's easy to relax when you know Lidia's* truc *for getting the clams to relax.*

Before opening clams, arrange them in a single layer in a pan and place in the freezer for 15 minutes. The intense cold relaxes the clams' muscles and makes opening them a snap.

#69
KEEPING LOBSTER TAILS UNCURLED

—

Lobster tails will curl when cooking. And that's fine, unless you have in mind an elaborate presentation requiring flat, uncurled lobster tails. Jean-Louis Palladin *frequently has that need, so he devised this* truc *for "lobster on a stick."*

To keep a lobster tail straight when cooking, insert a bamboo skewer through the back of the lobster tail and out the front. Remove the skewer when the lobster is cooked and the tail will stay straight.

#70
CRACKING A
LOBSTER CLAW

A whole lobster claw, neatly extracted from its shell in one perfect piece, is the height of elegant presentation. But shelling the claw in one neat piece requires one neat truc. *And* Hubert Keller's *got one.*

Break off the lobster claw from the body. Twist the small pincher and pull it off the claw. Using the heel of a chef's knife, crack the claw across its broad middle area. Twist the knife back and forth until the shell cracks and begins to break. Open the shell, and the claw meat will pull out easily in one piece.

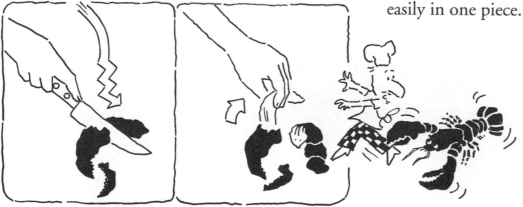

#71
KEEPING A LOBSTER ALIVE FOR A WEEK

Lobsters are sold live, and they should stay that way until cooked. Keeping them alive at home, though, requires a truc. *"It's easy if you've got a lobster tank," says Chef André Soltner. "But if you don't, just give the lobster a newspaper and keep it cool. It'll stay alive for at least a week."*

Soak several pieces of newspaper in a pan filled with cool water. Place the paper on a flat work surface and set the lobster on top. Roll the lobster up in the paper, enclosing it completely, and refrigerate. It will keep at least a week.

#72
CLEANING SOFT-SHELL CRABS

When soft-shell crabs are served in a restaurant, they're completely edible. But that's because the kitchen staff removed the three inedible parts—eyes, lungs, and apron before serving. "It's easy," says Emeril Lagasse. "Three steps, two fingers, and you're done."

First, use thumb and forefinger to pinch off the crab's eyes. Second, lift the pointed ends of the shell and pinch out the lungs—the saclike, spongy organs on either side. And third, turning the crab onto its back, pry up and pull off the flap, or apron. The crab is now fully cleaned, completely edible, and ready to cook.

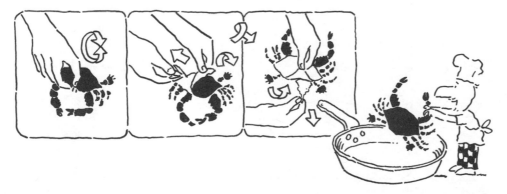

#73
ROUNDING OUT A SALMON CARPACCIO

Want a show-stopping presentation for smoked salmon? Present a perfectly round circle of salmon, perfectly centered on an elegant serving plate. How? Yannick Cam *reveals the* truc.

Place thinly sliced smoked salmon in the center of a serving plate. Place a piece of plastic wrap over the plate and brush it lightly with oil. Use the back of a spoon to press against the wrapped salmon, stretching the fish toward the rim of the plate. Place a second serving plate, identical to the first, on top of the fish, serving side up. Press down firmly and give the plate a twist. Remove the top plate, the plastic wrap and any scraps of fish from the edge of the plate. Garnish and serve.

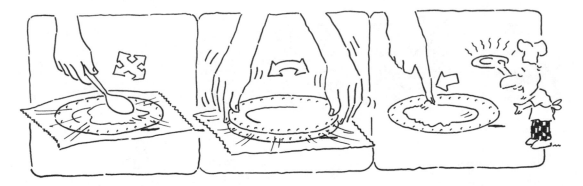

#74
FORMING THE PERFECT CARPACCIO OF TUNA

Diners at Charles Palmer's *restaurant marvel at the wide, thin, flat* carpaccio *of yellowfin tuna that emerges from his kitchen. How does he get the tuna that wide, that flat, that thin? "The* truc *involves ounces and pounds," says Charlie. "Three ounces of tuna, and many, many pounds."*

Put a piece of plastic wrap on a work surface and brush it lightly with olive oil. Place a 3-ounce piece of raw tuna on the plastic wrap, loosely folding the wrap over the fish. Using the flat side of a cleaver, slap the wrapped fish firmly, stretching the fish as it's pounded. After two or three pounds, turn the fish and pound again. Repeat this process until the tuna is completely flattened and very thin. Remove the plastic wrap and turn the *carpaccio* onto a plate. Serve chilled.

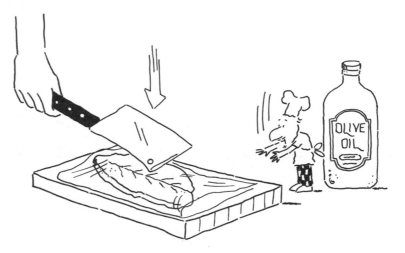

#75
BONING FISH

Chef Jacky Pluton *has an inspired* truc *for removing those pesky bones from raw fish fillets. It just takes a flick of the wrist and, of all things … a vegetable peeler!*

Run the peeler over the fillet, catching the bones in the center slit of the peeler. Twist the peeler slightly in the opposite direction and pull the bones right out.

#76
COOKING FISH IN PAPER

Cooking fish in a paper wrapper is a classic New Orleans technique that's ideal for such delicate fish as pompano, sole, and catfish. The concept is simple: fish, spices, and vegetables are sealed in a paper package and baked in a hot oven. The fish and vegetable juices, trapped within the package, provide flavorful steam that gently cooks the fish. The trick, of course, is in the bag—creating a package that holds in the steam. Emeril Lagasse shares a native truc *for sealing the paper so that the fish steams and cooks perfectly.*

Cut a circle from a heavy piece of cooking paper such as parchment or, preferably, butcher's wrap. (If neither is available, use aluminum foil.) Brush with melted butter or olive oil. Place the ingredients on one half of the circle, folding the other half over to cover. Seal the edges together with a series of small overlapping folds, working all the way around the paper. Twist the last fold several times, ensuring that the paper package, or *papillote,* is sealed tightly. Turn the *papillote* over and set it on a baking sheet. The fish is now ready to bake in its perfectly sealed package.

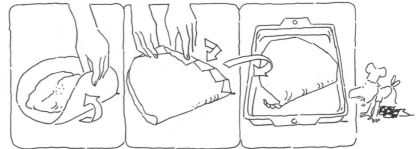

#77
FILLETING FRESH SALMON

Chef Hubert Keller *fillets a lot of salmon. He's developed a lightning-quick method that, according to conventional wisdom, is completely backward—he starts at the head of the fish.* "It's faster and easier," *says Hubert.* Vive la différence!

Start at the head end of the fish, not the tail. Cut around the gills until the knife hits the backbone. Then, holding the knife flat against the backbone, cut toward the tail using the backbone as a guide. With just one stroke, the entire side of salmon is filleted.

#78
SMOKING SEAFOOD
IN A SKILLET

Cold-smoking is an exotic technique for subtly flavoring food before cooking. It's an approach that works especially well with shrimp, scallops, and other mild seafood. The usual method is to fire up the grill and then make yourself crazy trying to regulate the heat so that it's hot enough to create smoke but not hot enough to cook the food. Jean-Michel Diot *has a low-tech, stove-top* truc *that's a lot less trouble.*

Place dried thyme sprigs in the bottom of a cold skillet. Top with fresh green thyme sprigs, then light the dried sprigs with a match. Place the seafood on a heavy china or Pyrex plate and set it on top of the burning herbs. Cover the skillet and let the seafood smoke for 30 minutes. Proceed to cook as usual.

BAKING AND DESSERTS

#79
ROLLING COLD DOUGH

"Most pastry recipes require that the dough be chilled thoroughly before rolling and baking. But rolling a cold dough is not easy," says Jacques Pépin. *He reveals a* truc *for making chilled dough so pliable that it can be rolled right after it's taken out of the refrigerator.*

Place the dough on the counter. With a rolling pin, pound the surface of the dough several times, making ridges. Place the rolling pin in the ridges and press down, spreading the dough slightly. Then turn the dough 90° and repeat the process until the dough is pliable and easy to roll.

#80
BAKING PIE SHELLS UPSIDE DOWN

It's one thing to put a perfectly shaped pie shell into the oven to bake; it's another to have it retain that perfect shape while baking. High heat causes the dough to contract and shrink as it bakes, and gravity causes it to slide down inside the pan. Jim Dodge *put gravity on his side, and developed this upside-down* truc *for baking a perfectly shaped pie shell.*

Start with two identical metal pie plates. Line one with pie dough that's been rolled into a sheet. Chill until the dough becomes firm to the touch. Set a second pie plate inside the dough-lined plate. Invert the plates onto a baking sheet, then bake. When the edge of the pie shell has turned a golden brown, the shell is baked. Take the baking sheet from the oven and turn the pie plates right side up, removing the inside plate.

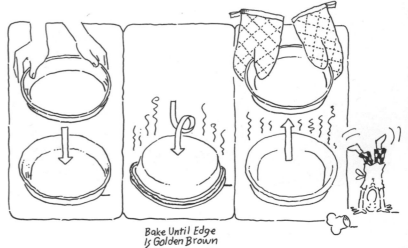

Bake Until Edge
Is Golden Brown

#81 5/25/96

REMOVING STUCK PARCHMENT PAPER FROM CAKES

As cakes cool after baking, they sometimes stick to their paper pan liners. Trying to remove the paper usually results in a tug-of-war that causes the cake to crumble. When Jacques Torres *encounters that kind of resistance, he brushes it aside with this clever* truc.

When parchment paper sticks to the bottom of a cake, brush the paper with a little warm water. After 10 to 20 seconds, the paper can easily be peeled right off the cake.

#82
CUTTING PAN LINERS

Perla Meyers *has been teaching baking classes in New York City for years. Her* truc *for cutting paper linings for cake pans, origami-style, has saved many of her students' cakes from sticking to the bottom of the pans.*

Take a piece of parchment paper large enough to cover the bottom of a cake pan. Fold the paper in half lengthwise, then crosswise. Fold diagonally to create a triangle. Fold the triangle in half lengthwise, forming a cone shape. Continue folding the cone shape lengthwise until it becomes quite narrow. Turn the cake pan over and place the tip of the paper cone at the center of the pan. With scissors, snip the paper where it meets the edge of the pan. Unfold the paper cone to reveal a circle that will perfectly fit the bottom of the cake pan.

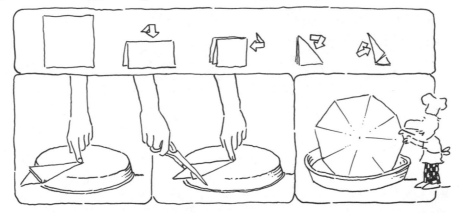

#83
ULTIMATE DISPOSABLE PASTRY BAG

Even a passionate baker like Rose Levy Beranbaum *doesn't like to wash pastry bags. So she set about to concoct a whole new disposable pastry bag system that makes cleanup unnecessary. Here's how:*

Take a heavy-duty zipper-seal plastic bag and snip off one corner, making a slightly curved cut. Using a standard two-piece plastic coupler (available wherever cake decorating supplies are sold), insert the larger piece into the hole.

Choose a tip and secure it with the coupler's ring. Fill the bag and zip the top closed. Decorate away, then remove the coupler/tip assembly and toss the bag. No messy cleanup!

#84
SWIRLING TWO COLORS FROM ONE PASTRY BAG

Swirling two different colors and flavors of mousse together makes for a dramatic visual and gustatory effect. Jacques Torres has a simple truc that employs two pastry bags to achieve one magical look.

To swirl two mousses together decoratively, scoop each mousse into its own pastry bag. Then slide both pastry bags, side by side, into one larger bag. Gather the larger pastry bag around the two smaller ones and squeeze. As the mousse emerges from the bag, it will appear swirled.

#85
BAKING REAL "CUP" CAKES

One of Mary Sue Milliken's most popular desserts is a "gourmet" version of an American snack favorite: the Hostess cupcake. In developing the recipe, Mary Sue sought to duplicate the rich, moist texture of the commercial version. The solution was in her cupboard. She discovered that to bake a rich, moist "cup" cake takes more than a good recipe—it also takes the right cup.

Butter and flour heavy, ovenproof porcelain coffee cups. Spoon cake batter into the cups, filling each two-thirds full. Bake in a preheated 325° oven for 20 to 25 minutes. Once baked, let the cakes cool slightly; then invert and pop them out of their cups.

#86
CRISPLY GLAZING CRÈME BRÛLÉE AT HOME

In restaurants, crème brûlée arrives at the table covered with a crisp, thin layer of caramelized sugar. But homemade versions of this classic usually lack this distinctive feature, having been made without the high-heat broilers found in restaurant kitchens. Hubert Keller *has solved the problem; he has a* truc *for creating a restaurant-style crème brûlée crust at home.*

First, go to a hardware store and buy a propane torch. Then, sprinkle a thin dusting of granulated sugar over the top of the crème brulée. Apply the lighted torch, keeping it several inches above the dish, moving the flame quickly back and forth. The sugar will melt, forming a thin, crisp crust.

#87
INSTANT CHOCOLATE DECORATOR

In The Cake Bible, *Rose Levy Beranbaum shares her secrets for making and decorating perfect cakes. None is more ingenious than what she calls her "instant chocolate decorator," an easily wrought pastry bag filled with piping chocolate.*

Put 1 cup of mini chocolate chips into a heavy duty zipper-seal plastic bag. Set the bag into a bowl of hot water for about 5 minutes, or until the chips melt. Pat the zipper-seal bag dry with a towel. Press the melted chocolate into one corner and zip the top closed. With scissors, clip off a small corner from the bottom of the bag. (Start small—you can always enlarge it.) Pipe away.

#88
MAKING CHOCOLATE RIBBONS

New York's Le Cirque is known for its impeccable service, its stellar food, and the stunning desserts created by its pastry chef, Jacques Torres. *Jacques's chocolate cake is topped with a deliciously delicate chocolate bow and festooned with chocolate ribbons. Jacques unwraps his* truc *for making this spectacular decoration.*

Cut a strip of cellophane (not plastic wrap) about 1½ inches wide. Place the cellophane strip on a cool table and brush it with melted chocolate, covering it. To make the bow, cut the strip into smaller lengths, 5 to 7 inches long. Working quickly, lift these strips and bring the two ends together to form a loop. When the chocolate hardens (this happens very quickly), peel off the cellophane and arrange several of these loops together on top of the cake to form a bow. Use the same technique to create the ribbons, forming them into flat or rippled shapes as desired.

#89
A BETTER WAY TO HUSK HAZELNUTS

Even a famous pastry chef like Jim Dodge *had about as much trouble as the rest of us in getting the skins off hazelnuts. Until, that is, he discovered the benefits of steam heat and developed this* truc *for removing those stubborn skins without endless rubbing.*

Place hazelnuts in a single layer on a cookie sheet and mist them with water. Bake in a preheated oven at 400° for 5 minutes. This small amount of water creates enough steam to loosen the skins so they slip right off the nuts.

#90
STRING-CUTTING CHEESECAKE

Rose Levy Beranbaum's mother is a dentist, which may explain why Rose uses dental floss instead of a knife to cut cheesecake. But it may just be that she uses dental floss because it does a superior job—quicker, neater, and better than a knife.

Cut a piece of dental floss several inches longer than the diameter of the cheesecake. Holding it taut, set the floss on the top surface of the cake. Press the floss right down through the cake until it reaches the bottom. Let go one end of the floss and pull it out through the other side of the cheesecake. Repeat this process to cut the desired number of slices.

#91
KEEPING IT IN THE BAG

"Nothing is more frustrating than loading up a pastry bag only to have the filling leak out through the tip," says Jim Dodge. *Jim's discovered a* truc *that keeps the filling in the bag "and out of your shoes."*

Twist the pastry bag just above the tip, making a knot. Press this knot into the tip and then fill the pastry bag. When the bag is filled, untwist the knot and squeeze the filling into the tip area.

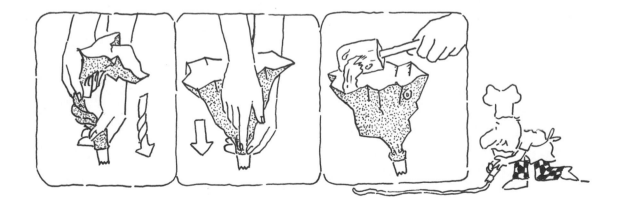

#92
RESTORING CURDLED CRÈME ANGLAISE

With its briefly cooked blend of egg yolks, cream, and sugar, crème anglaise may be the world's most popular dessert sauce. But if it's overcooked (and that's easy to do), the yolks curdle to create very sweet, very creamy scrambled eggs. Patrick Clark has a truc for repairing the curdled crème.

Pour the curdled crème into a blender and give it a 2-second jolt on high. The crème will regain its velvety smooth texture.

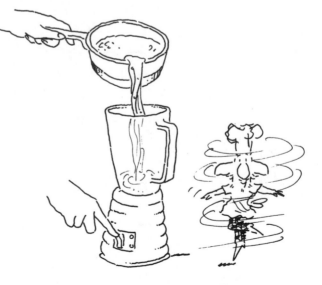

#93
FOOD PROCESSOR GRATING

———

Lots of dessert recipes call for grated lemon zest. This onerous task cannot be done in the food processor because the air currents from the blade causes the lightweight peel to fly around the bowl. Rose Levy Beranbaum *found that adding an abrasive ingredient to the workbowl solves the problem. Fortunately, most desserts call for this ingredient anyway.*

To grate zest in a food processor, add a small quantity of sugar. The sugar traps the peel and whirls it into the blades, resulting in a fine, powdery amalgamation of peel and sugar—perfect for desserts.

MISCELLANEOUS

#94
SHAVING PARMESAN CHEESE

Judy Rogers *adorns many of her soups, salads, and main dishes with wide, luxurious shavings of Parmesan instead of measly little gratings. Her razor? An ordinary vegetable peeler.*

Push a swivel-blade vegetable peeler across a large, flat piece of Parmesan cheese, letting the shavings fall directly on the food to be garnished. Vary the pressure, speed, and depth to achieve different-size shavings.

#95
SLICING DELICATE TERRINES

Nothing is more disheartening than watching a perfectly baked terrine crumble into pieces when it's sliced. Gerard Pangaud knows how to keep delicate terrines from breaking under the pressure of a knife. Here's his truc for guaranteeing a perfect slice.

Unmold the terrine and completely wrap it in a piece of aluminum foil. Place the wrapped terrine on a counter, steady it with one hand, and slice through the foil with a very sharp knife. Set the slice on a serving plate and remove the foil.

#96
PAN FRYING WITHOUT
HOT OIL SPLASHES

Maneuvering ingredients in a pan of sizzling oil can be a harrowing experience. All too often, the oil splashes on the cook and spills on the stove, inviting a fire. Larry Forgione *has a two-step* truc *to prevent this mayhem when pan frying.*

Place food in the skillet starting at the side nearest you, unfolding it away from you toward the back of the pan. That way, if any grease splashes, it will splash away from the cook. When it's time to turn the food, tilt the pan to one side, letting the hot oil slide in that direction. Turn the item over into the *drier* area of the pan. Then lay the pan flat, letting the oil once again cover the bottom, and continue cooking.

#97
THREE-HANDED COOKING USING ONLY TWO

When Patrick Clark *needs to pour with one hand, whisk with one hand, and steady a bowl with one hand—he keeps this* truc *close at hand … just in case no one else is.*

Twist a wet kitchen towel into a tight ring and wrap it around the base of the bowl. This will steady the bowl on the counter, leaving your hands free to pour and whisk simultaneously.

#98
PREVENTING BOIL-OVERS

Watched pots never boil. But unwatched pots do. And in a busy restaurant kitchen, they sometimes boil over. Mary Sue Milliken *doesn't worry about pots boiling over, because she knows this whisk* truc.

Keep a whisk next to the stove at all times. When a boil-over is imminent, plunge the whisk into the pot and beat rapidly. The bubbles will recede immediately, allowing enough time to remove the pot from the heat before its contents spill over.

#99
PAINTING WITH SAUCE

When it comes to getting sauce on a plate, most of us reach for a spoon, a ladle, or a sauceboat and simply pour it on. Jean-Jacques Rachou has a different approach. He "paints" the plate with sauces to create a variety of decorative effects. His signature look is a plate painted with intricate designs in sauces of contrasting colors, which serve as edible background for the food. It takes a special "paintbrush" to achieve this look—a dime-store squeeze bottle.

Fill a squeeze bottle with smooth, lump-free sauce and pipe designs directly onto the plate. Endless designs are possible by varying the color of the sauces, the size of the opening in the nozzle, and blending techniques (dragging the tip of a paring knife blade creates fanciful swirls). Experiment!

#100
SQUEEZING OUT THE OIL

"Coat lightly with olive oil" is a direction frequently employed in preparing such contemporary favorites as foccaccia or bruschetta, *meat, fish, or vegetables headed for the grill, or a bowl of greens needing a light dressing. But the truth is that coating lightly with olive oil is almost impossible using a pastry brush or even fingertips, the usual techniques.* Hubert Keller *has a better way—he squeezes it on.*

Fill a plastic squeeze-trigger bottle with olive oil. Holding the bottle 12 to 18 inches from the ingredients, give a couple of quick squeezes to provide a light, even coating of oil.

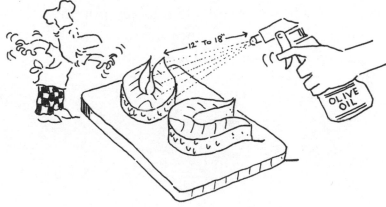

#101
QUICK-CHILLING
CHAMPAGNE

Champagne, the celebration beverage, is at its best served very cold, around 43°. In the average refrigerator, this takes well over an hour to achieve. But for those celebrations that just won't wait, Eileen Crane shares an ingenious professional truc *that does the job in 20 minutes flat. (For more modest celebrations, this* truc *works equally well with beer and white wines.)*

Fill an ice bucket half full of ice cubes. Pour in several cups of cold water and add 4 tablespoons of salt. Plunge the champagne into the ice bucket, adding additional water and ice to almost fill the bucket. Let sit for 20 minutes.

STARTERS

Avocado Dip. . . . . *Robert Del Grande*

Potato-Herb Wafers. . . . . *David Burke*

Tuna *Carpaccio* with Citrus Vinaigrette . *Charles Palmer*

Thinly Sliced Norwegian Salmon in a Corn Pancake
    with Golden Caviar . . . . *Hubert Keller*

Paillard of Salmon with Oyster Tartar . . . . *Jacky Pluton*

Carrot Soup with Dill. . . . . *Mary Sue Milliken*

Shoepeg Corn and Peanut Soup . . . . *Marcel Desaulniers*

Ancho and Navy Bean Soup. . . . . *Dean Fearing*

New England Fish Chowder. . . . . *Jasper White*

Bruschetta. . . . . *Pino Luongo*

Quail Eggs in Brioche with Caviar
    and Smelt Roe. . . . . *Jean-Louis Palladin*

Lobster with Snail Butter . . . . *André Soltner*

DRESSINGS AND SAUCES

Mayonnaise . . . . *André Soltner*

Roasted Tomatillo Salsa with Cilantro,
    Mint, and Avocado . . . . *Rick Bayless*

My Father's Vinaigrette. . . . . *Alain Sailhac*

Green Herb Oil . . . . *David Bouley*

RICE AND POLENTA

Perfect Rice. . . . . *Patrick Clark*

Artichoke-Flavored Rice . . . . *Felipe Rojas-Lombardi*

Basic Polenta . . . . *Lidia Bastianich*

ENTRÉES

Meat Dishes

The Arcadia Burger . . . . *Anne Rosenzweig*

Salad of Short Ribs and Beets
    with Tarragon. . . . . *Daniel Boulud*

Lamb Loin Chops with Mint Pesto
    and Artichokes. . . . . *Jimmy Schmidt*

Lamb Curry with Fried Onions . . . . *Susan Feniger*

Poultry Dishes

Roast Chicken à la *Truc*. . . . . *Michael Roberts*

Chicken *Boudin Blanc* . . . . *Michel Richard*

Chicken *Flautas* . . . . *Zarela Martinez*

Poblanos *Rellenos* . . . . *Zarela Martinez*

Pheasant in Chocolate Sauce . . . . *Felipe Rojas-Lombardi*

Seafood Dishes

Fried Soft-Shell Crabs with Crab Salad . . *Emeril Lagasse*

Lobster Tails with Squid Ink Pasta
    and Caviar Butter . . . . *Jean-Louis Palladin*

Roasted Lobster Packets with Coriander
    and Tomato *Coulis* . . . . *Hubert Keller*

Pompano Cooked in Paper . . . . *Emeril Lagasse*

Salmon Fillet Cooked on One Side Only . *Paula Wolfert*

Vegetarian Dishes

Lutèce's Famed Omelet. . . . . *André Soltner*

Eggplants Stuffed with Walnuts
    and Pomegranate Seeds. . . . . *Paula Wolfert*

Eggplants Filled with Pasta and Cheese *Lidia Bastianich*

DESERTS

Fleur-de-Lys's Crème Brûlée with Caramelized Apples
    and Orange Zest. . . . . *Hubert Keller*

Cordon Rose Cheesecake . . . . *Rose Levy Beranbaum*

Cupcakes, Hostess-Style . . . . *Mary Sue Milliken*

Tiny Fruitcake Gems . . . . *Rose Levy Beranbaum*

Espresso Chocolate and Hazelnut Cake
    with Brandy-Soaked Candied Fruit . . . . *Perla Meyers*

Balinese Mango Ice Cream with Rum . . *Craig Claiborne*

Upside-Down Pie Shell . . . . *Jim Dodge*

Dry-Poached Pears with Red Wine Sauce *Jimmy Schmidt*

Bartlett Pears in Puff Pastry. . . . . *Jacques Pépin*

STARTERS

AVOCADO DIP
▪ Robert Del Grande ▪

2 servings

¼ cup chopped yellow onion
4 cloves garlic, peeled (see Truc #11*)*
2 jalapeño peppers, stems removed
1½ cups water
2 tablespoons white wine vinegar
2 poblano chilies, peeled and seeded (see Truc #19*)*
⅓ cup toasted, shelled pumpkin seeds
2 avocados, peeled and pitted (see Trucs #2 *and* #3*)*
½ cup roughly chopped fresh cilantro (or to taste)
1 teaspoon salt (or to taste)
1 teaspoon coarsely ground black pepper

1. In a small saucepan, combine onion, garlic, and jalapeño peppers with the water and vinegar.

2. Bring the liquid to a boil and simmer for 15 minutes. Allow to cool.

3. Transfer the cooked ingredients and the liquid to a blender. Add the poblano chilies, pumpkin seeds, avocados, and cilantro, and purée for approximately 15 seconds. Do not overblend. Add the salt and pepper.

4. Let cool and serve with *crudités* and chips as a festive hors d'oeuvres.

POTATO-HERB WAFERS
▪ David Burke ▪

35 to 40 wafers

Two 2-inch copper pipes, the length of a cookie sheet
    (see Truc #25*)*
8 tablespoons (1 stick) unsalted butter
Two 6- to 7-ounce large baking potatoes, peeled
2 tablespoons finely chopped fresh herbs such as tarragon,
    cilantro, chives, sage, or basil (see Truc #55*)*
Coarse salt

1. Secure the copper pipes on a cookie sheet using crumpled aluminum foil to cradle the ends.

2. Melt the butter over low heat in a small saucepan. Remove from the heat and let sit until milky solids settle to bottom of the pan. Pour off the clarified butter and reserve.

3. Preheat oven to 325°.

4. Slice the potatoes on a mandolin so thinly that each slice is translucent. Soak the slices in the clarified butter.

5. Lay a potato slice over a pipe and sprinkle with approximately ½ teaspoon of chopped herbs. Then press another potato slice firmly against it, sealing the potato slices together and sandwiching the herb mixture in between.

6. Bake for 10 to 15 minutes, just until the potatoes are lightly brown and crisp. Season with salt and serve as a garnish or hors d'oeuvres.

TUNA CARPACCIO WITH CITRUS VINAIGRETTE

▪ CHARLES PALMER ▪

6 servings

Citrus Vinaigrette
½ cup extra-virgin olive oil
2 tablespoons freshly squeezed lemon juice (see Truc #31*)*
1 tablespoon freshly squeezed orange juice (see Truc #31*)*
1 tablespoon finely grated lemon zest (see Truc #34*)*
1 tablespoon white wine vinegar
1 tablespoon coarse salt
1 teaspoon freshly cracked white pepper
1 teaspoon chopped fresh chives
1 teaspoon chopped fresh parsley (see Truc #55*)*

Tuna
Six 3-ounce pieces center-cut yellowfin or bluefin tuna, ¼ to ½ inch thick
Olive oil for pounding
½ cup mixed salad greens

1. Prepare the vinaigrette by combining all the ingredients, except the chives and parsley. Whisk and refrigerate until ready to use. Just before serving, add the chives and parsley.

2. Place the tuna on a sheet of oiled plastic wrap and pound until thin—see *Truc #74*. Place the *carpaccio* on a serving plate with a bouquet of fresh salad greens. Spoon the vinaigrette over the tuna and greens and serve immediately.

THINLY SLICED NORWEGIAN SALMON IN A CORN PANCAKE WITH GOLDEN CAVIAR

▪ Hubert Keller ▪

6 appetizer servings

3 to 4 ears of corn, husked
3 eggs
2 tablespoons flour
Salt
Freshly ground pepper
1 cup watercress leaves
1½ teaspoons butter
1 tablespoon chopped shallots
1 tablespoon white wine
⅔ cup heavy cream
6 ounces filleted Norwegian salmon
    (see Trucs #75 and #77)
12 teaspoons (3 ounces) golden caviar
2 tablespoons vegetable oil
2 tablespoons sour cream
1 tablespoon chopped chives
18 cooked asparagus tips

1. *To make the pancake batter:* Bring 4 quarts of salted water to a boil. Add the corn and cook for 5 minutes, then immediately plunge into a bowl of cold water. Scrape the kernels off the cobs and set aside.

2. In a food processor, combine the corn, eggs, flour, a pinch of salt, and a few grindings of pepper. Process into a chunky purée. Check the seasonings, adding more salt and pepper if necessary. Set aside.

3. *To make the watercress sauce:* Wash the watercress leaves under cool water. Simmer the leaves in boiling salted water for 3 minutes; plunge into cold water to stop the cooking and then squeeze out the moisture with your hands.

4. Melt the butter in a small saucepan over medium heat. Add the shallots and sauté until golden. Stir in the white wine and simmer until the moisture evaporates. Add the cream. Bring to a boil, then lower the heat and simmer for 5 minutes. Add the watercress leaves and cook for 1 minute. Season with salt and pepper. Keep warm.

5. *Prepare the salmon:* Slice the fillet into 6 thin slices. Put them flat on a plate and top each with a teaspoon of caviar. Fold the salmon over the caviar so that the caviar is sealed inside. Season the salmon with salt and pepper.

6. Heat the oil in a skillet over medium heat. Drop about 1½ tablespoons of pancake batter into the pan. Top with a scallop of salmon, then spoon another 1½ tablespoons of pancake mixture over the salmon, just to cover. Cook 4 to 6 pancakes at a time, turning them once.

7. *To assemble:* Spoon the warm watercress sauce into the center of a plate. Place a pancake in the center of the sauce and top with 1 teaspoon of sour cream, 1 teaspoon of caviar, and a sprinkling of chopped chives. Decoratively place 3 asparagus tips around the plate. Repeat for the remaining pancakes. Serve warm.

PAILLARD OF SALMON WITH OYSTER TARTAR

▪ JACKY PLUTON ▪

4 servings

Olive oil
1½-pound salmon fillet, cut into four 6-ounce pieces (see Truc #75)
8 oysters
3 tablespoons finely chopped shallots
2 teaspoons finely chopped capers
1 teaspoon Tabasco sauce
1 teaspoon Worcestershire sauce
1 heaping tablespoon finely chopped chervil or parsley leaves (see Truc #55)
1 hard-boiled egg
Salt

Freshly ground pepper
¼ cup lemon juice
Warm toast

1. Brush a 12-inch-square piece of plastic wrap with olive oil. Place 1 piece of salmon on the wrap and fold it over the salmon. Using the flat side of a meat cleaver, pound the salmon, pressing it out until it is about ¼ inch thick and forms a rectangle approximately 6 × 4 inches.

2. Heat a large skillet and cook the salmon paillard for 20 seconds over medium-high heat; turn it over and cook it for another 10 seconds. Cook all the salmon, then set aside.

3. *For the tartar,* open the oysters and set their juice aside. Finely chop the muscle. Combine the chopped oysters with the shallots, capers, Tabasco sauce, Worcestershire sauce, chervil, and reserved oyster juice.

4. Separate the egg white from the egg yolk. First press the egg white and the yolk through a fine sieve (see *Truc #40*). Set aside in separate piles.

5. Sprinkle a plate decoratively with salt and pepper. Lay a salmon paillard on the plate and brush with olive oil and lemon juice. Place a spoonful of oyster tartar in the center of the salmon paillard. Fold the salmon over, pocketing the tartar in the middle. Sprinkle the edge of the fish with egg white and egg yolk. Repeat with remaining salmon. Serve paillard cold with warm toast.

CARROT SOUP WITH DILL
▪ Mary Sue Milliken ▪

4 to 6 servings

2 tablespoons unsalted butter
¾ cup sliced onions
2 teaspoons salt
½ teaspoon white pepper
1 bunch fresh dill
4 cups chicken stock or canned broth (see Truc #60)
1 pound carrots, peeled and finely chopped (3½ to 4 cups)
1 cup heavy cream
1 cup half-and-half

1. Melt butter over medium-low heat in a large stockpot or Dutch oven. Cook onions with salt and pepper until soft, about 5 minutes.

2. Chop dill in half, crosswise, separating the leaves from the stems. Reserve the leaves for garnish. You should have about 1 cup. Tie the stems with string and place in the pot (see *Truc #54*). Add the chicken stock and cook over medium heat, uncovered, about 15 minutes.

3. Remove and discard the dill stems and add the carrots. Bring to a boil, lower heat to a simmer, and cook, uncovered, until the carrots are soft, about 10 minutes.

4. Purée the soup in a blender or food processor until smooth. Strain back into the pot, pressing with the back of a ladle to extract all juices. Add the cream and half-and-half. Bring to a boil and remove from the heat. Serve immediately, garnished with dill leaves.

SHOEPEG CORN AND PEANUT SOUP
▪ Marcel Desaulniers ▪

8 servings

6 cups Vegetable Stock (recipe follows)
1 cup (about 5 ounces) shelled, unsalted Virginia peanuts, skinned
7 tablespoons safflower oil
1 tablespoon water
1½ cups diced celery
½ cup diced onions (see Truc #16)
Salt
Freshly ground pepper
2 cups (about 2 ears) white shoepeg corn (or other variety) kernels
½ cup all-purpose flour
4 tablespoons creamy peanut butter

1. Prepare Vegetable Stock. Cool.

2. Preheat the oven to 300°.

3. Spread the peanuts on a cookie sheet and roast them in the oven for 25 to 30 minutes, until golden brown. Set aside.

4. Heat 1 tablespoon of the oil and the water in a 5-quart sauce pan over medium heat. Add the celery and onions, cook for 5 minutes. Season with salt and pepper. Add the corn kernels and sauté for 5 minutes. Add the Vegetable Stock and bring to a boil. Reduce heat and simmer for 15 minutes.

5. In a small saucepan, heat the remaining oil over low heat, add the flour and stir. Add the peanut butter and blend. Cook for 6 minutes, stirring constantly so that the peanut butter won't scorch.

6. Add 4 cups of the soup's broth to the peanut butter mixture, whisking vigorously until smooth. Whisk this mixture into the soup and blend. Simmer for 10 minutes. Season with salt and pepper to taste.

7. To serve, sprinkle the roasted peanuts over the soup.

VEGETABLE STOCK

8 cups

3 quarts water
2 medium onions, chopped (1 cup) (see Truc #16)
4 stalks celery, chopped (1½ cups)
1 medium potato (about 4 ounces), peeled and cut into 1-inch pieces
2 leeks, white part only, chopped (½ cup)
1 medium carrot, washed and chopped (¾ cup)
1 medium tomato, cored and chopped (½ cup) (see Truc #26)
1 teaspoon salt
2 medium garlic cloves, peeled (see Truc #11)
1 teaspoon chopped fresh parsley
½ teaspoon whole black peppercorns

1. Heat ½ cup of the water in a 5-quart saucepan over medium-high heat. Add the onions, celery, potatoes, leeks, carrots, tomato, and salt. Cover and steam for 5 minutes.

2. Add remaining water, garlic, parsley, and peppercorns. Bring liquid to a boil, reduce heat, and simmer for 2 hours.

3. Strain the stock and cool (see *Truc #60*). Stock can be refrigerated for 2 days or frozen for up to 1 month.

ANCHO AND NAVY BEAN SOUP

• DEAN FEARING •

4 servings

2 cups dried white navy beans, picked over and rinsed
4 thick slices smoked bacon
1 large onion, peeled and chopped (see Truc #16*)*
1 stalk celery, trimmed and chopped
2 large shallots, peeled and chopped
2 cloves garlic, peeled and chopped (see Truc #11*)*
2 serrano chilies, chopped
4 cups Ham Stock (recipe follows)
4 cups chicken stock
1 cup Ancho Chili Paste (recipe follows)
Salt
Freshly squeezed lime juice (see Truc #31*)*
1 red onion, peeled and cut into ¼-inch dice (see Truc #16*)*
8 fresh cilantro leaves (see Truc #51*)*

1. Cover navy beans with at least 8 cups of cold water. Allow to soak at least 8 hours. Drain well.

2. Render fat from bacon in a large stockpot over medium heat. Add onion, celery, shallots, garlic, and serrano chilies and sauté for 3 minutes. Add beans, Ham Stock, and chicken stock. Bring to a boil, reduce heat, and simmer for 40 minutes.

3. When done, combine soup and Ancho Chili Paste in a blender and purée until smooth. Stir in salt and lime juice to taste. Strain and recheck seasoning. Pour soup into 4 warm soup bowls and garnish with red onion and cilantro leaves just before serving.

HAM STOCK

4 cups

2 tablespoons bacon fat
1 large onion, peeled and chopped (see Truc #16*)*
2 stalks celery, trimmed and chopped
1 carrot, chopped
1 bunch fresh cilantro, chopped (about ¾ cup)
2 jalapeño peppers seeded and chopped (see Truc #23*)*
1 pound ham bones
1 pig's foot
1 bay leaf
1 tablespoon chopped fresh or 1½ teaspoons dried thyme leaves
1 teaspoon whole black peppercorns
4 quarts cold water

1. Heat bacon fat in a large saucepan over medium-high heat. Add onion, celery, carrot, cilantro, and jalapeño peppers and sauté for 4 minutes or until transparent. Do not brown the vegetables.

2. Add ham bones, pig's foot, bay leaf, thyme, and peppercorns. Cover with the water and bring to a boil. Lower heat and simmer for 4 hours.

3. Strain stock through a fine sieve, discarding solids, and cool quickly (see *Truc #60*). Refrigerate for up to 2 days or freeze for up to 1 month.

ANCHO CHILI PASTE

1 cup

1 cup chicken stock
4 ancho chilies, seeded (see Truc #22)
1 small onion, peeled and chopped (see Truc #16)
1 clove garlic, peeled and chopped (see Truc #11)
1 small bunch fresh cilantro (about 10 sprigs)

1. Place all the ingredients in a small saucepan over medium heat. Simmer for 10 minutes.

2. Pour into a blender and purée until smooth. Cool quickly (see *Truc #60*). Set aside until ready to use, or refrigerate for up to 2 days or freeze for up to 1 month.

NEW ENGLAND FISH CHOWDER
• JASPER WHITE •

8 to 10 servings

3½ pounds fresh cod fillets, skinned
¼ pound meaty salt pork, cut in ¼- to ½-inch dice
12 tablespoons unsalted butter
3 cups diced onions, cut into ¾-inch dice (see Truc #16)
3 bay leaves
1 tablespoon chopped fresh thyme leaves
3 or 4 large Maine or other boiling potatoes, peeled and cut lengthwise in half, then into ¼-inch slices
3 cups strong Fish Stock (recipe follows) (see Truc #57)
2 cups heavy cream
Salt
Freshly ground black pepper
2 tablespoons chopped fresh parsley and/or chervil (see Truc #55)

1. Prepare the fish by removing any excess skin and picking out any bones with a pair of tweezers. If you use a knife to cut out bones, be sure to leave the fillets in as large pieces as possible.

2. Render the fat from the salt pork, medium-high, in a large soup pot until it begins to crisp. Add 4 tablespoons of the butter, the onions, bay leaves, and thyme. Cook for 5 minutes until the onions become soft. Add the potatoes and Fish Stock and simmer for 20 minutes, until the potatoes are tender.

3. Remove the bay leaves and add the cod fillets and heavy cream. Simmer slowly until the fish is cooked through and begins to flake (about 8 to 10 minutes). Season to taste with salt and pepper. Stir in the chopped parsley. Remove from heat.

4. Using a slotted spoon, transfer the chunks of fish, the onions and potatoes to soup plates, then ladle over the piping hot broth. Put a dollop of butter into each plate of soup and serve with crackers or biscuits.

FISH STOCK

8 cups

2½ to 3 pounds fish bones
2 tablespoons unsalted butter
1½ cups finely chopped leeks
1 cup finely chopped onions (see Truc #16*)*
1½ cups finely chopped celery
1½ cups thinly sliced carrots, peeled
3 bay leaves
2 sprigs thyme
4 or 5 parsley stems (see Truc #54*)*
½ teaspoon whole black peppercorns
1 cup dry white wine
Salt (optional)

1. Cut the fish bones into pieces 2 to 3 inches across. Trim the bones of any excess skin or viscera that may still be attached. Rinse or soak if necessary in cold water to remove completely any traces of blood.

2. Melt the butter in a stockpot over low heat and add the leaks, onions, celery, carrots, bay leaves, thyme, parsley stems, and peppercorns. Cook for about 5 minutes, stirring a few times.

3. Add the wine and place the fish bones on top of the vegetables. Cover the pot and allow the bones to sweat in the aromatic steam. After 20 minutes, remove the lid and pour in 4 cups of water, enough to cover the fish bones.

4. Raise the heat and bring the stock to a boil. Skim the top, then reduce the heat to a slow simmer. Simmer for 10 minutes and remove from the heat. Allow the stock to sit for another 10 minutes. If you like, you can lightly salt the stock.

5. Gently strain the stock through a fine strainer and chill as quickly as possible (see *Truc #60*). Freeze any leftover stock for up to 1 month.

BRUSCHETTA

• PINO LUONGO •

2 servings

3 ripe plum tomatoes, cored and diced small (about ¾ cup)
   (see Truc #27*)*
Salt
Freshly ground pepper
2 basil leaves, cut into fine ribbons (see Truc #55*)*
3 tablespoons olive oil
Two ¾-inch-thick slices crusty peasant bread
1 medium clove garlic, peeled (see Truc #11*)*

1. In a bowl, combine the tomatoes, salt and pepper to taste, basil, and 1½ tablespoons of oil. Set aside.

2. Toast the bread lightly on both sides.

3. Slightly bruise the garlic clove and rub it over the perimeter of the bread, using the crusty edge to grate the garlic (see *Truc #15*).

4. Drizzle the bread using 1½ tablespoons of olive oil. Sprinkle with salt.

5. Toss the tomato mixture to blend and spoon onto the warm bread. Serve immediately.

QUAIL EGGS IN BRIOCHE WITH CAVIAR AND SMELT ROE

• JEAN-LOUIS PALLADIN •

4 servings

8 to 10 quail eggs
8¼-inch-thick slices brioche
Vegetable oil
Freshly ground black pepper
2 ounces mixed caviar (about 2 teaspoons each of beluga,
   ossetra, American golden caviar, and smelt roe) or 1¼
   ounces (about 8 teaspoons) smelt roe
½ teaspoon minced fresh chives (optional)

SPECIAL UTENSILS:
Two or more cookie cutters of assorted geometric shapes,
   each about equal in area to a 3-inch-round cookie cutter,
   for cutting brioche into shapes
One 1-inch round cookie cutter
Cookie sheet or baking pan large enough to hold 8 brioche
   shapes and also fit under broiler

1. Heat oven to 400° and preheat broiler, if you have a separate broiler unit. *(continued)*

2. Open the quail eggs (see *Truc #41*), setting the opened eggs in an "egg carton" fashioned from crumpled aluminum foil. Set aside.

3. Use the larger cookie cutters to cut out 8 geometric shapes of brioche, then use the smaller round cutter to cut out a hole in the center of each.

4. Oil the cookie sheet and heat it in the oven, about 1 minute. Remove cookie sheet from oven (leave oven on) and arrange the brioche shapes on it in a single layer. Gently pour the quail eggs into the center holes of the shapes. Return cookie sheet, uncovered, to the oven and bake for 2 minutes; then immediately broil for just a few seconds, about 4 inches from the heat source, until brioche is lightly toasted and egg whites are opaque (the yolks should still be very runny). Remove from broiler. Season tops with pepper.

5. *To assemble:* Transfer 2 brioche shapes to each of 4 heated serving plates. With 2 teaspoons, mold the caviar or smelt roe into 8 quenelles (oval shapes) allowing about 1 level teaspoon of caviar and/or smelt roe for each. As each is formed, place on top of one of the brioche shapes, next to the egg. Sprinkle with chives, if desired. Serve immediately.

Note: You will need 8 eggs for this recipe, but it's a good idea to have extras in case any break.

LOBSTER WITH SNAIL BUTTER
• ANDRÉ SOLTNER •

2 appetizer servings

2 tablespoons unsalted butter, softened
1 tablespoon chopped parsley (see Truc #55*)*
2 tablespoons chopped shallots
1 clove garlic, peeled and chopped (see Truc #11*)*
¼ teaspoon salt
Freshly ground pepper
1 tablespoon Pernod or Ricard
1¼-pound live lobster (see Truc #71*)*

1. *To make the snail butter:* In a food processor, combine the butter, parsley, shallots, garlic, salt, pepper, and liqueur. Set aside.

2. Preheat the oven to 450°.

3. With a sharp knife, split the lobster in half, lengthwise. Discard the stomach (the small sac behind the eyes) and the intestinal vein.

4. Place the lobster in a round shallow gratin dish and cover with snail butter. Roast in a very hot oven for 10 minutes and serve immediately.

Note: There are no snails in the snail butter; André calls it *snail* butter because it is the same butter that he uses to cook snails at Lutèce.

DRESSINGS AND SAUCES

MAYONNAISE
▪ ANDRÉ SOLTNER ▪

1 quart

4 large egg yolks (room temperature)
1½ teaspoons Dijon mustard
1 teaspoon white vinegar
Pinch of salt
White pepper to taste
4 cups vegetable oil (room temperature)

1. Whisk egg yolks together with mustard, vinegar, salt, and pepper.

2. Begin to add oil slowly, a few drops at a time, while continuing to whisk vigorously. After the mayonnaise emulsifies and begins to thicken, the oil can be added a little more quickly.

3. Continue whisking until all the oil is incorporated and the mayonnaise is thick and smooth. Adjust seasoning, if necessary.

Note: If at any point the mayonnaise breaks—loses its texture and becomes runny—see *Truc #62.*

ROASTED TOMATILLO SALSA WITH CILANTRO, MINT, AND AVOCADO
▪ RICK BAYLESS ▪

1¾ cups

½ pound (about 5 or 6) fresh tomatillos (Mexican green tomatoes), husked and washed
1 jalapeño pepper or 2 serrano chilies, stemmed, halved, and deveined, seeds reserved (see Truc #23)
½ small onion, finely chopped (¼ cup) (see Truc #16)
3 tablespoons vinegar
6 sprigs fresh cilantro, finely chopped (2 tablespoons)
2 small sprigs mint, finely chopped
1 avocado, pitted, peeled, and diced (see Trucs #2 and #3)
½ teaspoon salt

1. Preheat broiler.

2. Place the tomatillos on a cookie sheet and roast them 6 inches below the broiler, turning them gently as they blister and brown on all sides. Set aside to cool.

3. In a food processor, roughly chop the jalapeño pepper. Add the tomatillos and process into a smooth purée. Transfer to a small mixing bowl.

4. Put the onion in a small strainer and dip several times into a bowl of water mixed with about 3 tablespoons of vinegar. This rinses away the souring juices (see *Truc #17*). Shake off excess water and add to the bowl of tomatillos along with the cilantro, mint, and avocado. If the salsa is too thick, add ¼ cup water. Season with salt. Let the salsa sit for 30 minutes before serving.

Note: In Southwestern cooking, tomatoes, tomatillos, garlic, and green peppers are frequently roasted to blacken their peels and intensify their flavor. This roasting is accomplished either under a broiler, as in this recipe, or in an iron skillet over high heat, as in Zarela Martinez's recipe for Roasted Tomato Sauce (page 153).

MY FATHER'S VINAIGRETTE
▪ ALAIN SAILHAC ▪

2 servings

1 medium garlic clove, peeled (see Truc #11*)*
1 teaspoon Dijon mustard
1 tablespoon red wine vinegar
Dash of salt
13 twists of the pepper mill
3 tablespoons olive oil

1. Grate the garlic with the tines of a fork (see *Truc #13*). Add the mustard, vinegar, salt, and pepper. Blend together, using the fork. Very slowly add the olive oil, whisking all the while.

2. Toss with salad greens just before serving.

GREEN HERB OIL
▪ DAVID BOULEY ▪

1 cup

⅓ cup extra virgin olive oil
⅓ cup vegetable oil
One 500-milligram vitamin C tablet
½ cup chopped fresh leafy green herbs—basil, parsley, tarragon, or cilantro (see Truc #55*)*

1. Combine the oils in a blender and place in freezer until very cold, about ½ hour.

2. Crush the vitamin C tablet into a fine powder. Combine with the oil and blend until the tablet is dissolved (see *Truc #56*).

3. Add the herbs and blend until the leaves are fully puréed and emulsified in the oil.

4. Store in the refrigerator.

RICE AND POLENTA

PERFECT RICE

• PATRICK CLARK •

4 servings

1 cup rice
2 teaspoons vegetable oil
1 cup water or stock

1. In a saucepan, over medium heat, sauté the rice in the oil until the individual grains are coated and just beginning to turn opaque, about 1 minute.

2. Add water or stock and bring to a boil. Stir rice, cover, and reduce heat to a simmer.

3. Cook for 10 minutes, then remove from heat. Do not uncover. Let sit for 15 minutes, then remove lid. Fluff the rice with a fork and serve (see *Truc #45*).

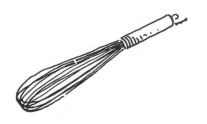

ARTICHOKE-FLAVORED RICE

• FELIPE ROJAS-LOMBARDI •

6 servings

1 tablespoon olive oil
1 or 2 cloves garlic, peeled and crushed (see Truc #11*)*
2 cups long-grain rice
4 cups water or stock
1 large artichoke, quartered
Coarse salt to taste

1. In a saucepan, heat the oil over low heat. Add the garlic and sauté until lightly browned on all sides, about 4 minutes. Do not burn the garlic.

2. Remove the garlic, add the rice, and sauté for about 5 minutes.

3. Add 4 cups water and the artichoke quarters; bring to a boil over high heat (see *Truc #48*). Cover the pan tightly, reduce heat to low, and simmer for 10 to 12 minutes, or until rice has absorbed all the liquid.

4. Remove the artichoke quarters, and fluff the rice with a fork. Season with salt and serve.

BASIC POLENTA

▪ Lidia Bastianich ▪

4 servings

*4 cups cold water (2 cups milk plus 2 cups water can be
    used for a richer taste)*
1 tablespoon unsalted butter
1 bay leaf
2 tablespoons coarse salt
1½ cups coarse yellow cornmeal

1. Place the water in a medium-size cast-iron saucepan
or other heavy pot. Add the butter, bay leaf, and salt.

2. Very slowly, begin to sift the cornmeal into the pan
through the fingers of one hand, stirring constantly with
a wooden spoon or whisk. (This operation will be greatly
facilitated if the meal is scooped by the handful from a
wide bowl.) Gradually sift all the meal into the pan (see
Truc #44).

3. Place the pan over high heat and stir until the mixture begins to simmer. Then reduce heat to medium-low
and cook, stirring constantly, until the polenta is smooth,
thick, and pulls away from the sides of the pan as it is
stirred, about 30 minutes. Discard the bay leaf. Pour the
polenta into a serving bowl or onto a wooden board, and
allow it to rest for 10 minutes.

4. To serve from the bowl, dip a large spoon into hot
water and scoop the polenta onto individual dishes, dipping the spoon into the water between scoops. To serve
from the board, cut the polenta into segments with a thin,
taut string or a knife and transfer to plates with a spatula
or cake server. The polenta can also be fried or grilled.
Serve as a side dish with stews, poultry, and seafood.

ENTRÉES

MEAT DISHES

THE ARCADIA BURGER

▪ Anne Rosenzweig ▪

8 servings

Herb Butter
8 tablespoons butter
1 tablespoon finely chopped fresh thyme leaves
2 tablespoons finely chopped fresh basil leaves (see Truc #55)
1 tablespoon chopped fresh parsley leaves (see Truc #55)

Hamburgers
6 pounds freshly ground chuck (20 to 22% fat)
Herb Butter
Salt
Freshly ground pepper
16 ½-inch-thick slices Italian peasant bread
1½ cups olive oil
16 to 24 slices ripe tomato
16 thin slices red onion
1 cup freshly squeezed lemon juice (see Truc #31)

1. Make the Herb Butter by softening the butter and combining with the chopped herbs. Shape into a log, wrap in plastic wrap, and freeze. To use, slice into 8 pieces.

2. Divide the meat into 8 balls, touching it only lightly as you work. Make an indentation in each ball and press a nugget of herb butter into the meat (see *Truc #63*). Close the indentation and shape the meat into patties about 1 inch thick. Season with salt and pepper. Grill over medium flame, about 4 minutes on each side.

3. Brush the bread slices on one side, using ½ cup of the olive oil. Place the slices, oiled side down, on the grill and lightly toast. Turn over and toast the other side.

4. Combine the tomato and onion slices in a bowl with the remaining olive oil, the lemon juice, and salt and pepper to taste.

5. Serve the burgers on the grilled bread, with the tomato-onion salad offered as a topping.

SALAD OF SHORT RIBS AND BEETS WITH TARRAGON

▪ DANIEL BOULUD ▪

4 to 6 servings

4 pounds thick beef short ribs
4 leeks, rinsed well (separate greens from whites)
1 carrot, peeled and split in half
1 teaspoon celery salt
¼ teaspoon crushed black peppercorns
1½ teaspoon salt
1 pound beets, cleaned (see Truc #6)
½ pound small redskin potatoes, scrubbed, but not peeled
1 teaspoon finely chopped shallots
1 clove garlic, peeled and chopped (see Truc #11)
3 tablespoons chopped parsley leaves (see Truc #55)
1 tablespoon chopped fresh tarragon leaves
5 tablespoons of red wine vinegar
8 to 10 tablespoons olive oil
Salt
Freshly ground pepper
1 head Boston lettuce
⅓ cup fresh chives, cut into 1-inch pieces

1. Place the short ribs in a Dutch oven and cover with 4 quarts of water.

2. Add the leek greens, carrot, celery salt, crushed black pepper, and 1½ teaspoons of salt. Boil gently for 1 hour.

3. In a separate pot, boil the beets in water until done (60 minutes minimum).

4. Remove the short ribs from their pot, strain the bouillon, discard the vegetables (or keep them for soup), and return the ribs and bouillon to the Dutch oven.

5. Add the potatoes and the leek whites and bring to a boil. Cook for another 30 to 45 minutes, then drain. (Quickly cool and refrigerate the cooking bouillon to use in sauces or as a soup. See *Truc #60.*)

6. Cut the meat in ½-inch slices. Discard the bones and the fat.

7. Slice the potatoes into ¼-inch dice and quarter the leek whites. In a bowl, toss the meat and vegetables together while still warm.

8. Add the shallots, garlic, 2 tablespoons of the parsley, and 1 teaspoon of the tarragon. Sprinkle with 3½ tablespoons of the vinegar, 5 to 7 tablespoons of the olive oil, and salt and freshly ground pepper to taste. Toss carefully to avoid mashing the vegetables.

9. Drain the beets, cool, peel and cut into thin wedges. Season with the remaining parsley and tarragon, 1 tablespoon of the vinegar, 2 tablespoons of the olive oil, and salt and freshly ground pepper to taste.

(continued)

10. Toss the lettuce with the remaining vinegar and olive oil. Place the lettuce leaves on the bottom and around the sides of a large salad bowl. Place the short rib mixture in the center of the lettuce and surround with the beet mixture. Sprinkle the salad with chives.

LAMB LOIN CHOPS WITH MINT PESTO AND ARTICHOKES

▪ JIMMY SCHMIDT ▪

4 servings

Salt
4 medium artichokes
6 cloves garlic, roasted and minced
¾ cup olive oil
Eight 4-ounce lamb loin chops
1 cup chopped fresh mint leaves
½ cup chopped fresh parsley leaves
¼ teaspoon freshly ground black pepper
1 tablespoon Balsamic vinegar
¼ cup fresh whole mint leaves

1. Bring 4 quarts of water to a boil in a large saucepan. Add 2 tablespoons salt and the artichokes. Cook until tender, about 45 minutes. Test for doneness by inserting a skewer through the base of the artichoke. When tender, drain the water and set the artichokes aside to cool.

2. Once the artichokes are cool enough to handle, quarter them, remove the hearts, and set aside (see *Truc #1*).

3. In a small mixing bowl, blend one third of the garlic with 2 tablespoons of the olive oil. Rub the mixture over the surface of the lamb chops.

4. Preheat the broiler or grill.

5. In a food processor or blender, combine the remaining garlic and olive oil with the chopped mint and parsley and pepper. Process until finely chopped, then add the vinegar. Season with salt to taste. Set aside at room temperature.

6. Broil the chops for 5 minutes, turn them and continue broiling for another 4 minutes—they will be medium-rare.

7. *To serve:* spoon mint pesto over each chop. Garnish with whole mint leaves and the quartered artichoke hearts.

LAMB CURRY WITH FRIED ONIONS

▪ SUSAN FENIGER ▪

6 servings

4 pounds boneless, trimmed lamb shoulder
Salt
Freshly ground pepper
1 cup vegetable oil
1½ cups diced onions (see Truc #16*)*
2 tablespoons puréed garlic (see Truc #14*)*
2 tablespoons black mustard seeds
2 tablespoons garam marsala
2 teaspoons turmeric
2 teaspoons ground cardamom
2 teaspoons ground cumin
1 teaspoon dried red pepper flakes
2 quarts brown lamb stock or canned chicken broth
4 cups cooked white rice (basmati preferred)
1 cup plain yogurt
Fried Onions (recipe follows)

1. Cut meat, as uniformly as possible, into 2 × 3-inch cubes. Generously sprinkle with salt and pepper.

2. Heat oil in a large Dutch oven over high heat. Cook meat until golden on all sides; reserve on a platter.

3. In the same pot, cook the diced onions, stirring occasionally, until golden. Reduce heat to medium, add garlic and all dry spices, and cook 3 minutes, stirring constantly.

4. Return the meat to pan and pour in stock. Bring to a boil, reduce heat to a simmer, and cook, uncovered, 1 hour and 15 minutes. Occasionally skim and discard the fat that rises to top.

5. Ladle warm stew over a bed of white rice. Garnish with yogurt and Fried Onions. Serve immediately.

FRIED ONIONS

6 servings

1 large onion
¼ cup vegetable oil

1. Peel the onion and slice it as thinly as possible—more like a shave than a cut—across the width. (You may need to use a meat slicer or food processor fitted with a 1-millimeter blade to slice it this fine.)

2. Heat the oil over moderate heat in a small skillet. Working in small batches, fry the onion, constantly shaking the pan, until crispy and golden, about 3 minutes.

3. Remove the slices with tongs or a slotted spoon and drain on paper towels.

POULTRY DISHES

ROAST CHICKEN À LA TRUC

▪ Michael Roberts ▪

4 servings

One 4- to 5-pound roasting chicken, seasoned with salt and
*   pepper*
⅓ cup olive oil, melted butter, margarine, or chicken fat
4 tablespoons all-purpose flour
¼ cup dry white wine
1½ cups chicken stock or canned low-sodium chicken broth

1. Preheat the oven to 425°. Place the bird, breast side down, in a roasting pan and place in the oven. Reduce the heat to 350° and roast for 10 minutes.

2. Soak a double layer of cheesecloth (large enough to cover the chicken) with the olive oil. Set aside (see *Truc #65*).

3. Turn the bird breast side up and cover with the cheesecloth. Return to oven and roast 60 minutes, basting with pan juices every 15 minutes. (When well cooked, the thigh will move freely in its joints.)

4. Remove the bird from the pan and place on a serving platter.

5. Set the roasting pan on the stove over medium heat. With a wooden spoon, stir in the flour. Add wine and broth and bring to a simmer, scraping up concentrated juices that cling to the bottom of the pan. Reduce the broth by one-third. Check seasoning. Pour the gravy into a sauce boat.

6. Untruss the bird and serve immediately, with gravy.

CHICKEN BOUDIN BLANC

▪ MICHEL RICHARD ▪

6 servings

¾ cup finely chopped onion (see Truc #16)
2 cups heavy cream
1 pound boneless skinned chicken breast, cut into chunks
¼ teaspoon freshly grated nutmeg
½ teaspoon salt
3 drops Tabasco sauce
4 large eggs
Plastic wrap (see Truc #64)

1. Simmer the onions in the heavy cream over low heat for 30 minutes. Stir occasionally to prevent scorching. Strain cream into a small bowl, discarding the onions. Set bowl in an ice bath to cool cream.

2. In a food processor, purée the chicken with the cooled cream, nutmeg, salt, and Tabasco sauce. Once the mixture is smooth, add the eggs and continue to process.

3. Lay 3 feet of plastic wrap on the counter. Fit a pastry bag with a ½-inch tube. Fill the bag with the chicken mixture (see *Truc #91*). Pipe chicken mixture on the plastic wrap, beginning 3 inches up from the long edge. Pipe so the sausage is 1 inch in diameter.

4. Roll the sausage tightly, tying each end with a piece of string. Pinch the sausage roll at 6-inch intervals, tying each pinch with a piece of string.

5. Drop the sausage roll into a pot of barely simmering water. Poach for 30 minutes, until the sausage firms up. Once cooked, plunge immediately into a bowl of iced water to cool.

6. Refrigerate until ready to serve. Before serving, unwrap the sausages and pan fry in a lightly oiled nonstick pan until the sausages turn a golden brown. Serve hot.

CHICKEN FLAUTAS

▪ ZARELA MARTINEZ ▪

4 to 6 servings

2 tablespoons lard or oil
½ cup finely chopped onion (see Truc #16)
1 teaspoon minced garlic (see Truc #11)
3 cups shredded poached chicken meat
Salt
Freshly ground pepper
16 corn tortillas (see Truc #49)
Vegetable oil for frying

1. Heat the lard in a skillet over medium heat. Add the onions and garlic and cook until translucent, about 3 minutes. Add the chicken, stir well, season with salt and pepper to taste, and cook for 5 minutes.

2. *To prepare the flautas:* Soften tortillas in the microwave, four at a time. Lay them flat on the counter and place 2 tablespoons of chicken mixture in the center of each. Roll each into a tight cylinder, securing it with a toothpick. Place the rolled tortillas in a plastic bag until you are ready to cook.

3. *To cook:* Pour 3 inches of oil into a deep saucepan. Heat to 350°. Fry 2 or 3 flautas at a time until golden, about 5 minutes. Drain on a plate lined with paper towels. Serve hot with salsa or guacamole.

POBLANOS RELLENOS

▪ ZARELA MARTINEZ ▪

6 servings

½ cup pimiento-stuffed green olives
½ cup each pitted prunes, dried apricots, and dried peaches
6 large poblano chilies
Vegetable oil for frying
8 tablespoons (1 stick) unsalted butter
¾ cup chopped onion (see Truc #16)
2 garlic cloves, peeled and minced (see Truc #11)

1½ teaspoons ground cumin
½ teaspoon Cassia cinnamon (or 1½ teaspoons Ceylon cinnamon, more popular in Mexico)
¼ teaspoon ground cloves
2 cups shredded cooked chicken
Salt
Roasted Tomato Sauce (recipe follows)

1. Preheat the oven to 425°.

2. Slice the olives and coarsely dice the dried fruit. Set aside.

3. Make a slit in each of the poblano chilies (do not cut through) and fry in hot oil to remove the peel (see *Trucs* #19 and #96). Seed the chilies and set them aside.

4. Melt the butter in a large skillet over medium heat. Add the onions and garlic and sauté for 3 minutes. Stir in the olives and dried fruit and sauté for another 3 minutes. Add the spices and chicken and cook for 2 minutes, stirring. Season with salt to taste.

5. Spoon the chicken mixture into the peppers through the slit. Place the stuffed chilies on an oiled baking pan and bake for 7 minutes. Spoon the Roasted Tomato Sauce onto a serving plate and arrange the poblanos *rellenos* on top.

ROASTED TOMATO SAUCE
(SALSA DE TOMATE ASADO)

1½ cups heavy cream
8 cloves of garlic, unpeeled
1 medium onion, unpeeled and cut crosswise
2¾ pounds (about 3 to 4 large) tomatoes
Salt

1. In a small saucepan, simmer the cream until reduced to 1 cup.

2. Heat a heavy cast-iron skillet over high heat until it is hot to the touch. Roast the garlic and onion in the pan. Turn them several times until the garlic is dark on all sides and has softened, and the onion is partly blackened. Set aside.

3. Roast the tomatoes the same way until they blister on all sides. Let cool.

4. Peel the garlic, onion, and tomatoes and put in a blender. Purée on medium until smooth. Add the cream and blend until mixed. Season with salt. Return to the saucepan and simmer gently over low heat. Serve warm.

PHEASANT IN CHOCOLATE SAUCE
▪ Felipe Rojas-Lombardi ▪

6 to 8 servings

Two 2½-pound pheasants, each cut into 8 serving pieces
1 cup olive oil
2 cloves garlic, peeled and minced (see Truc #11)
1 or 2 fresh jalapeño peppers, seeded and minced (see Truc #23)
2 cups chopped onions (see Truc #16)
2 tablespoons chopped unsweetened chocolate
4 stalks celery, deveined and cut on the diagonal into ¼-inch slices (about 2 cups)
4 carrots, peeled and cut into ¼ inch slices (about 2 cups)
¼ cup all-purpose flour
1 tablespoon coarse salt
2 quarts chicken stock
4 links Morcilla sausages (or other blood sausages), skinned and chopped
3 wine corks (see Truc #66)

1. Pat the pheasant pieces dry and set aside.

2. Heat the oil in a sauté pan over medium-high heat. Brown the pheasant pieces evenly on all sides. Remove the pheasant from the pan and set aside. Discard all but ¼ cup of the oil.

3. Reduce the heat to medium-low and add the garlic, jalepeño peppers, and onions. Cook until the onion turns golden, about 10 minutes.

4. Add the chocolate and cook 2 minutes, then add the celery and carrots. Raise the heat to medium and cook for another 3 minutes.

5. Sprinkle the flour over the vegetables and stir until they are coated. Season with salt and add 2 cups of stock. Bring the stock to a boil, stirring constantly. Reduce the heat, and simmer for 5 minutes.

6. Add the pheasant, sausages, remaining stock, and the wine corks. Return to a boil, then reduce the heat and simmer for 30 to 45 minutes, until the pheasant is tender.

7. Once cooked, remove the corks and season with salt if necessary. Serve over white rice.

SEAFOOD DISHES

FRIED SOFT-SHELL CRABS WITH CRAB SALAD

■ EMERIL LAGASSE ■

4 servings

2 cups all-purpose flour
2 eggs
1 cup milk
1½ cups dry bread crumbs
2 tablespoons Creole Seasoning (recipe follows)
Four 5- to 6-ounce jumbo soft-shell crabs, cleaned (see Truc #72)
Vegetable oil
Creole Tomato Sauce (recipe follows)
Crab Salad (recipe follows)

1. Put the flour into a shallow pan, set aside. Combine the eggs with the milk in a shallow pan, set aside. In a third shallow pan, toss the bread crumbs and Creole Seasoning together.

2. Dredge the crabs in the flour, shaking off any excess. Dip crabs into the milk mixture and, finally, dredge them in the seasoned bread crumbs.

3. Deep fry the crabs in 375° oil for 2 minutes, just until the crabs turn golden. Remove and drain on paper towels.

4. *To serve:* Pool the Creole Tomato Sauce on the bottom of each plate. Put one soft-shell crab on top of the sauce, along with ½ cup Crab Salad.

CREOLE SEASONING

7 tablespoons

2½ tablespoons salt
2 tablespoons sugar
2 tablespoons freshly ground pepper
1 tablespoon cayenne

1. Combine all ingredients and mix thoroughly. Pour into a glass jar and seal tightly.

2. Creole Seasoning keeps indefinitely. Use the remainder to season grilled chicken, fish, and meat.

CREOLE TOMATO SAUCE

4 servings

6 medium tomatoes
2 tablespoons unsalted butter
¼ cup dry white wine
½ cup finely chopped onion
½ cup chopped fresh cilantro leaves (*see* Truc #55)
3 tablespoons Creole Seasoning (recipe precedes)
Freshly ground pepper to taste
Salt to taste

1. Preheat broiler.
2. Place tomatoes on a foil-lined baking sheet and roast, turning frequently, until skin has blistered and turned black (see *Truc #29*). Cool, remove skin, and chop tomatoes.
3. Melt the butter in a skillet over medium-high heat. Add wine and cook for 30 seconds.
4. Add tomatoes and remaining ingredients and simmer for 4 to 5 minutes, until the sauce thickens slightly. Keep warm until ready to serve.

CRAB SALAD

4 servings

2 cups water
½ cup packaged crab boil
1 tablespoon salt
½ teaspoon whole black peppercorns
1 clove garlic, peeled (*see* Truc #11)
2 ears corn
2 scallions, sliced (*see* Truc #18)
2 teaspoons Creole Seasoning (recipe precedes)
1 cup diced red bell pepper (*see* Truc #20)
2 tablespoons olive oil
2 tablespoons freshly squeezed lemon juice (*see* Truc #31)
1 pound jumbo lump crabmeat

1. In a saucepan combine the water, crab boil, salt, peppercorns, and garlic. Bring to a boil. Add the corn and simmer for 2 minutes. Remove the corn and cool.
2. Scrape the corn kernels from the ears and reserve.
3. In a bowl combine the corn kernels, scallions, Creole Seasoning, and red bell pepper. Using a fork, toss together. Add the olive oil and lemon juice and mix thoroughly.
4. Gently fold the crabmeat into the salad. Refrigerate until ready to serve. (No longer than 1 day in advance.)

LOBSTER TAILS WITH SQUID INK PASTA AND CAVIAR BUTTER

▪ JEAN-LOUIS PALLADIN ▪

4 servings

½ cup unsalted butter
½ cup pressed caviar
2 lobster tails, in shell
2 cups lobster consommé or fish broth (see Truc #57)
½ pound fresh squid ink pasta (black pasta)
4 sprigs chervil

1. To prepare the caviar butter, combine the butter and caviar in a food processor and process until well mixed. Refrigerate until firm, about 2 hours.

2. Insert a wooden skewer at the back of each lobster tail, pressing it out the front (see *Truc #69*). Poach the tails in the consommé until the meat is cooked, approximately 6 minutes. Reserve poaching liquid.

3. Remove both the shell and skewer from each lobster tail and cut each crosswise into 8 slices. Cover with a kitchen towel and reserve.

4. Cook the pasta in boiling, salted water. Prepare the sauce by combining ¼ cup of the poaching liquid with the caviar butter in a saucepan. Do not overheat or the sauce will separate.

5. *To serve:* Pile the pasta high in the center of each plate. Arrange slices of lobsters around the mound of pasta and ladle on some of the caviar butter sauce. Top each with a sprig of chervil and serve.

ROASTED LOBSTER PACKETS ON A CORIANDER AND TOMATO COULIS

▪ HUBERT KELLER ▪

4 servings

Bouquet garni (made with bay leaf, thyme, and parsley)
Salt to taste
Freshly ground pepper to taste
Two 1¼-pound live lobsters (see Truc #71)
⅔ cup heavy cream
2 medium leeks, chopped
1 tablespoon chopped chives
12 large spinach leaves
2 tablespoons olive oil
1 tablespoon chopped shallots
1 small garlic clove, peeled and finely chopped (¼ teaspoon)
　(see Truc #11)
3 large tomatoes, peeled, seeded, and diced (2 cups)
　(see Truc #27)
¼ teaspoon sugar or to taste
1 tablespoon finely chopped fresh cilantro leaves (see Truc
　#55)

4 quail eggs (see Truc #41)
Chopped fresh chervil leaves, for garnish (see Truc #55)

1. Line a 1½-quart casserole, 9 × 13 inches, with parchment paper.

2. *To cook the lobsters:* Bring 6 quarts of water to a boil in a large stockpot. Add bouquet garni, salt, pepper, and lobsters. Poach for 8 minutes. Remove the lobsters and cool. Break each lobster's tail off where the tail meets the body. With scissors, cut off the soft underpart of the tail, then remove the meat in one piece. Remove the claw meat, also in one piece (see *Truc #70*). Set the meat aside.

3. Bring the cream to a boil in a medium saucepan. Add the leeks and season with salt and pepper. Reduce heat, cover and simmer for 6 to 8 minutes or until the leeks become tender. Add the chives and set aside to cool.

4. Quickly blanch the spinach leaves in lightly salted boiling water, set aside.

5. Dice the lobster meat and add to the cream mixture. Toss to blend.

6. Preheat the oven to 350°.

7. Lay the spinach leaves flat on the counter. Spoon the lobster mixture into the center of each spinach leaf. Fold each leaf around the lobster mixture, creating an envelope. Arrange the stuffed leaves, seam side down, in the prepared casserole. Sprinkle the leaves with 1 tablespoon of the olive oil and roast for 6 minutes.

8. *To make the tomato* coulis: Heat the remaining olive oil in a small saucepan. Add the shallots and cook until golden. Add the garlic and tomatoes, then season with salt, pepper, and sugar to taste. Reduce heat and simmer for 5 minutes, until the tomato *coulis* thickens. Add the cilantro and adjust seasonings.

9. *To serve:* Spoon 1 tablespoon of tomato *coulis* into the center of each plate. Arrange 3 lobster packets around the sauce. Cook the quail eggs, sunny-side up, and place one in the center of each plate. Sprinkle with chervil.

POMPANO COOKED IN PAPER

▪ EMERIL LAGASSE ▪

4 servings

¼ cup olive oil
4 tablespoons unsalted butter
½ cup thinly sliced fresh basil leaves (see Truc #55*)*
Four 12-ounce pompano fillets
¼ cup Creole Seasoning (page 155)
8 medium plum tomatoes, cut into ½-inch slices
1 onion, cut into ¼-inch slices

1. Preheat the oven to 450°.

2. Cut 4 pieces of parchment paper into large heart shapes. Lay the hearts flat on the counter. Brush half of each heart with olive oil and then dot with a tablespoon of butter.

3. Sprinkle half the basil evenly over the oiled paper. Place a fish fillet on top of the basil, then season with Creole Seasoning. Top the fish fillets with remaining basil.

4. Make a single layer of tomatoes on top of each fish fillet and then top with a single layer of onions.

5. Fold the paper over the fish. Seal the fish inside by making a series of overlapping folds around the perimeter (see *Truc #76*). Twist the last fold several times to ensure that the paper packages are completely sealed.

6. Place the paper-wrapped fish on a baking sheet and bake for 10 to 15 minutes. When the paper package balloons and browns, the fish has steamed inside.

7. Bring the fish to the table in their paper packages, letting guests open their own. A wonderful aroma will waft from the fish as the packages are opened.

SALMON FILLET COOKED ON ONE SIDE ONLY

▪ PAULA WOLFERT ▪

2 servings

¾ *pound center-cut fresh Atlantic salmon fillet, skin on*
1 *tablespoon olive oil*
½ *teaspoon sea salt*
2 *teaspoons unsalted butter*
8 *small capers, rinsed, drained, and chopped*
3 *tablespoons sliced scallions, white part only (see* Truc #18)
1 *ripe tomato, peeled, seeded, and cut into ¼-inch cubes*
   (about ⅔ cup) (see Truc #27)
3 *tablespoons cubed lemon flesh, with rind, pith, and seeds*
   removed (see Truc #32)
Salt
Freshly ground pepper
2 *tablespoons shredded fresh sorrel leaves (see* Truc #55)
2 *tablespoons snipped chives*

1. Cut the salmon crosswise into 2-inch-wide strips. Lightly brush with olive oil and sprinkle with sea salt. Place the salmon, skin side down, on a heated, well-seasoned iron skillet or griddle and cook over low heat for 20 minutes *without turning*. Use a dome lid or foil to cover the salmon for the last 5 minutes to finish the cooking. (Note that the color of the salmon will not turn dull and the texture will be very juicy.) Scrape off any globules of fat and reserve.

2. Meanwhile, melt the butter in a small skillet, add the capers and scallions and cook, stirring, 1 minute. Add the tomato and lemon and cook 30 seconds. Season to taste with salt and pepper. Swirl in the reserved salmon fat.

3. Raise the heat under the large skillet to crisp the skin of the fish at the last minute. Serve the salmon, skin side down, with the warm tomato garnish, sorrel, and chives.

VEGETARIAN DISHES

LUTÈCE'S FAMED OMELET

▪ ANDRÉ SOLTNER ▪

1 serving

1 tablespoon kosher salt (approximately)
3 eggs
Table salt
1 tablespoon butter
Freshly ground pepper

1. Sprinkle kosher salt into omelet pan and rub vigorously with a paper towel. Discard salt (see *Truc #42*).

2. Crack the eggs into a bowl and beat vigorously with a fork until the whites and yolks are thoroughly blended. Once the eggs are pale yellow in color and well beaten, add a sprinkling of table salt.

3. Add the butter to the pan and let it melt over high heat. Roll the butter around the pan, coating the bottom. Give the eggs one last quick beating with a fork and then pour them into the pan. Using a fork, stir and fold the eggs while they cook. Be careful not to overcook them, otherwise they become rubbery.

4. Once the eggs have cooked, tilt the pan over a serving plate and slide the eggs toward the edge of the pan. Fold the top of the eggs into the middle, and continue rolling toward the bottom of the pan. Flip the eggs onto the plate. Straighten the omelet, so that it is cigar-shaped. Season with a few grindings of pepper.

EGGPLANTS STUFFED WITH WALNUTS AND POMEGRANATE SEEDS

▪ PAULA WOLFERT ▪

4 to 6 servings

1¾ teaspoons salt
8 to 10 baby eggplants, halved lengthwise (see Truc #10)
2 cups coarsely chopped walnuts
1 garlic clove, peeled and minced (see Truc #11)
½ teaspoon hot Hungarian paprika
¼ teaspoon ground turmeric
⅓ cup chopped celery leaves
¼ cup shredded fresh basil leaves (see Truc #55)
⅓ cup chopped fresh cilantro leaves (see Truc #55)
¼ cup minced red onion
2 tablespoons rice wine vinegar
¼ cup pomegranate seeds (see Truc #37)
1½ tablespoons olive oil
Italian parsley for garnish

1. Sprinkle 1 teaspoon of the salt over the cut side of the eggplants. Place them, flat side down, on paper towels. Set a plate on top of the eggplants, weighing them down for 20 minutes. Rinse the eggplants under cool water and gently squeeze out the moisture. Pat dry with paper towels. Set aside.

2. Place the remaining salt, the walnuts, garlic, paprika, and turmeric in a food processor. Process until mixture becomes an oily paste. Add ⅓ cup of water and process to blend. Transfer the paste to a mixing bowl and stir in the celery leaves, basil, cilantro, onion, and vinegar. Fold in the pomegranate seeds. Cover with plastic wrap and set aside.

3. In a 9-inch skillet, heat the olive oil over medium-low heat. Add the eggplant, flat side down. Cover tightly and cook until the flesh is golden and the eggplant is tender, about 15 minutes. Transfer the eggplant to paper towels to drain and cool slightly.

4. With your fingers, split open the flesh of the cut side of the eggplant. Mound the walnut filling into the slit and serve warm or at room temperature. Garnish with parsley and extra pomegranate seeds.

EGGPLANTS FILLED WITH PASTA AND CHEESE
(TUBETTINI ALLA SICILIANA)

▪ LIDIA BASTIANICH ▪

4 servings

Four 6- to 8-ounce round male eggplants (see Truc #10)
3 tablespoons olive oil
½ cup cooked pasta, such as ditalini or tubettini
8 ounces mozzarella cheese, diced
2 tablespoons grated Parmesan cheese
Salt
Freshly ground pepper
½ cup tomato sauce

1. Preheat oven to 375°.

2. Wash the eggplants and cut off the tops. Scoop out the pulp and mince it, reserving the shells.

3. Heat 2 tablespoons of the olive oil in a skillet over medium heat. Add the eggplant pulp and cook, covered, for 5 minutes. Stir the pulp occasionally.

4. Combine eggplant pulp with pasta, mozzarella cheese, a sprinkle of Parmesan cheese, salt and pepper to taste, and the remaining olive oil.

5. Add enough tomato sauce to moisten the pulp mixture. Blend well. Mound the filling in the eggplant shells. Top with remaining tomato sauce and Parmesan cheese.

6. Bake for 30 minutes, or until golden.

DESSERTS

FLEUR-DE-LYS'S CRÈME BRÛLÉE WITH CARAMELIZED APPLES AND ORANGE ZEST

▪ Hubert Keller ▪

6 servings

3 cups heavy cream
The grated zest of 1 lemon (see Truc #34)
The grated zest of 1 orange (see Truc #34)
9 large egg yolks
¼ cup granulated sugar
3 tablespoons butter
2 large Granny Smith apples, peeled and sliced into 15 slices each
¼ cup packed light brown sugar

Special Utensil:
Propane torch

1. Preheat the oven to 275°. Butter the sides and bottoms of 6 shallow 4-ounce crème brûlée molds. Set aside.

2. In a saucepan, bring the cream and lemon and orange zests to a boil.

3. Meanwhile, whisk together the egg yolks and granulated sugar. Once the cream comes to a boil, remove from heat and gradually add it to the egg yolk mixture, whisking constantly.

4. Fill the prepared molds with the crème brulée mixture and set them in a roasting pan. Place the pan in the oven and add enough boiling water to reach halfway up the sides of the molds. Bake for 40 minutes.

5. Melt the butter in a sauté pan over high heat. Add the apple slices and sauté until brown and slightly softened. Set aside.

6. When the crème brulée is firm, remove from the oven and water bath. Fan five apple slices over the top of each mold. Sprinkle with brown sugar.

7. With a propane torch, melt the brown sugar (see *Truc* #86). When the crème brulée cools slightly, it will have a thin, crispy crust. Serve warm or at room temperature.

CORDON ROSE CHEESECAKE

▪ ROSE LEVY BERANBAUM ▪

8 to 12 servings

Two 8-ounce packages cream cheese, at room temperature
1 cup sugar
1 tablespoon cornstarch
3 large eggs
3 tablespoons freshly squeezed lemon juice (see Truc #31)
1½ teaspoons vanilla extract
¼ teaspoon salt
3 cups sour cream

SPECIAL UTENSIL:
Dental Floss

1. Preheat the oven to 350°. Butter an 8 × 2½-inch springform pan and line the bottom with greased parchment or wax paper.

2. In a large mixing bowl beat the cream cheese and sugar until very smooth (about 3 minutes), preferably with a whisk beater.

3. Beat in the cornstarch if desired. Add the eggs, one at a time, beating after each addition until smooth; scrape down the sides of the bowl. Add the lemon juice, vanilla, and salt and beat until incorporated. Beat in the sour cream, just until blended.

4. Pour the batter into the prepared pan. Set the pan in a larger pan and surround it with 1 inch of very hot water. Bake 45 minutes. Turn off the oven. Without opening the door, let the cake cool for 60 minutes. Remove to a rack and cool to room temperature (about 60 minutes). Cover with plastic wrap and refrigerate overnight.

5. *To unmold:* Have ready a serving plate and one flat plate at least 8 inches in diameter, covered with plastic wrap. Place pan on heated burner and move it around for 15 seconds. Wipe the side of the pan with a hot, damp towel.

6. Run a thin metal spatula around the side of the cake and release the side of the springform pan. Place the plastic-wrapped plate on top and invert. Remove the bottom of the pan and the parchment paper. Reinvert the cake onto the serving plate and use a small metal spatula to smooth the side. Refrigerate until shortly before serving.

7. *To cut:* Use the dental floss method (see *Truc #90*).

Note: For a richer, denser cheesecake that completely holds its moisture without cornstarch, replace the 3 whole eggs with 6 egg yolks.

An 8 × 3-inch solid cake pan can be used instead of a springform. To unmold the cake, run a thin spatula around the side, place the pan on heated burner for 10 to 20 seconds, moving the pan back and forth, and then invert. If the cake does not release, return to the hot burner for a few more seconds.

CUPCAKES HOSTESS-STYLE

▪ Mary Sue Milliken ▪

18 cupcakes

5 ounces unsweetened chocolate, chopped
1 cup packed brown sugar
1 cup milk
4 large egg yolks
8 tablespoons butter
1 cup granulated sugar
2 cups all-purpose flour
1 teaspoon salt
1 teaspoon baking soda
¼ cup heavy cream
1 teaspoon vanilla extract
3 large egg whites
2½ cups Pastry Cream (recipe follows)
¾ cup Ganache (recipe follows)
½ cup Pure White Frosting (recipe follows)

1. Preheat oven to 325°. Butter and flour a 12-cup and a 6-cup muffin tin, or prepare 18 ovenproof porcelain cups (see *Truc #85*).

2. Melt the chocolate in the top of a double boiler or in a bowl over simmering water. In another bowl, combine brown sugar, ½ cup of the milk and 2 of the egg yolks. Whisk until combined. Add to melted chocolate and cook over simmering water, stirring constantly, until mixture is shiny and thick, about 3 minutes. Set aside to cool.

3. In a clean bowl, cream the butter and granulated sugar until light. Add the remaining 2 egg yolks, one at a time, beating well after each addition.

4. In another bowl, mix together flour, salt, and baking soda.

5. Combine cream, vanilla, and remaining ½ cup milk in a small bowl and reserve.

6. Pour the cooked chocolate mixture into the butter and sugar mixture. Whisk until smooth. Add the cream mixture and dry ingredients in three stages, alternating liquid and dry ingredients, and ending with liquid.

7. Beat the egg whites until soft peaks form. Gently fold, all at once, into the batter. Spoon the batter into the muffin cups, about two-thirds full.

8. Bake 20 to 25 minutes, until a toothpick inserted in center comes out clean. Set aside to cool, in the pan, on rack, about 10 minutes. Invert and set aside on a lined sheet pan to cool, about 60 minutes. Prepary Pastry Cream, Ganache, and Pure White Frosting.

9. Using the tip of a small paring knife, cut a small cone from the bottom of each cupcake. Reserve cones. Scoop out about 1 teaspoon of cake from the center of each cupcake. Fill a pastry bag fitted with a plain tip with Pastry

Cream (see *Truc #91*). Pipe the cream into cupcakes, then replace the reserved cones. Place the cupcakes bottom-side down on a lined sheet pan and chill.

10. When the Ganache has cooled, dip the cupcakes in to coat the tops. Fill a plain-tipped pastry bag with Pure White Frosting (see *Truc #91*) and decorate each cupcake with a squiggle across the top, Hostess-style. Store in the refrigerator until serving time (up to 1 day).

PASTRY CREAM

2½ cups

½ cup sugar
¼ cup cornstarch
4 large egg yolks
2 cups milk
½ teaspoon vanilla extract

1. Mix ¼ cup of the sugar and the cornstarch in a bowl until smooth. Add the egg yolks and mix until a paste is formed. Stir in ½ cup of the milk.

2. Combine the remaining milk and sugar in a saucepan and bring to a boil. Pour the hot mixture into the bowl with the egg yolks, whisking constantly. Pour back into the saucepan.

3. Cook over moderate heat, stirring constantly, until smooth and thick. Remove from heat and stir an additional minute. Stir in the vanilla and transfer to a bowl. Cover with buttered parchment paper that touches top of the cream and chill a minimum of 2 hours (up to 2 days).

GANACHE

¾ cup

3 ounces semisweet chocolate, chopped
⅓ cup plus 1 tablespoon heavy cream

1. Place chocolate in a medium bowl.

2. Bring cream to a boil and pour into the chocolate. Stir until chocolate is completely melted.

3. Let cool until mixture is less than body temperature.

PURE WHITE FROSTING

½ cup

⅔ cup confectioners' sugar
1 tablespoon milk

1. Mix in a small bowl until smooth.

TINY FRUITCAKE GEMS

▪ Rose Levy Beranbaum ▪

3½ dozen

8 tablespoons unsalted butter
½ cup small mixed candied fruit
2 tablespoons candied citron
¼ cup dried currants
¼ cup pecan halves
½ cup Myer's dark rum
½ cup unsifted cake flour, without leavening
¼ teaspoon cinnamon
¼ teaspoon salt
⅛ teaspoon baking soda
¼ cup packed dark brown sugar
1 large egg
¼ liquid cup unsulfured molasses (preferably Grandma's)
2 tablespoons milk
1 teaspoon vanilla extract
¼ cup minced candied cherries, optional

1. Place the oven rack in the center of the oven and preheat the oven to 325°. Set the tartlet tins on a baking sheet so that the edges don't touch.

2. Soften the butter with the beater of an electric mixer, set aside.

3. Finely chop the candied fruit, citron, currants, and pecans. Put them in a small mixing bowl and combine with ¼ cup of the rum. Set aside.

4. In another small mixing bowl, combine the flour, cinnamon, salt, and baking soda. Set aside.

5. In a large mixing bowl, cream the butter and brown sugar together until light and fluffy. Beat in the egg and gradually add the flour mixture in 3 batches, alternating with the molasses and milk. Add the candied fruits (with the soaking rum) and the vanilla, then beat until blended.

6. Scrape the batter into a 1-gallon zipper-seal plastic freezer bag. Cut a small piece from one of the corners of the bag. Pipe the batter into the tartlet molds, filling them three-quarters full (see *Truc #83*).

7. Bake 15 to 17 minutes, or just until the batter begins shrinking away from the sides of the molds and the top springs back when lightly touched.

8. Unmold the gems on a buttered piece of wax paper. Brush the tops with the remaining rum. As an option, place ¼ teaspoon of minced candied cherries in the center of each gem. Once cooled, wrap each in a small piece of plastic wrap.

ESPRESSO CHOCOLATE AND HAZELNUT CAKE WITH BRANDY-SOAKED CANDIED FRUIT

▪ PERLA MEYERS ▪

10 servings

Cake
¼ cup finely minced excellent-quality candied fruit
¼ cup brandy
8 ounces bittersweet chocolate (preferably Lindt)
5 tablespoons strong prepared coffee mixed with 1 teaspoon instant espresso
8 tablespoons unsalted butter, cut into pieces and chilled
3 extra-large eggs, separated
⅔ cup granulated sugar
4½ tablespoons cake flour
⅔ cup ground hazelnuts (see Truc #89)
Whipped cream

Glaze
3 ounces bittersweet chocolate (preferably Lindt)

2 tablespoons strong prepared coffee
1 tablespoon confectioners' sugar
3 tablespoons unsalted butter, cut into pieces and chilled

1. Preheat the oven to 375°.

2. Butter the inside of an 8-inch round cake pan, preferably one with a high, straight side or a springform. Cut a piece of parchment paper to fit bottom of pan (see *Truc #82*). Butter the parchment paper. Sprinkle the pan lightly with flour, shaking out the excess, and set aside.

3. *To make the cake:* In a small bowl, combine the candied fruit with the brandy and let macerate for at least 60 minutes.

4. In the top of a double boiler, combine the chocolate and 5 tablespoons of coffee, set over warm water, and stir until smooth. Remove from heat, let cool slightly, and whisk in 8 tablespoons of butter, 1 tablespoon at a time, until completely incorporated. Reserve.

5. Combine the egg yolks with ½ cup of the granulated sugar in a large mixing bowl and beat until fluffy and pale yellow. Add the chocolate mixture and whisk until just blended. Add the flour, hazelnuts, and candied fruit and brandy mixture and fold gently but thoroughly.

6. In a large bowl, combine the egg whites with the remaining granulated sugar and beat until they hold firm peaks. Fold the beaten whites gently but thoroughly into the chocolate and hazelnuts, being careful not to deflate the mixture. Pour the batter into the prepared cake pan.

7. Place the pan in the center of the oven and bake for 20 minutes. Remove the cake from the oven and let it sit on a wire cake rack for 15 minutes. Run a knife around the inside of the cake pan, if necessary, and invert the cake onto a serving platter. Carefully peel off and discard the parchment paper (see *Truc #81*). Let the cake cool for 6 hours or refrigerate overnight.

8. *To make the glaze:* Combine the chocolate, 2 tablespoons of coffee, and the confectioners' sugar in the top of a double boiler set over warm water and stir until smooth. Remove from heat, cool slightly, and stir in 3 tablespoons of butter, 1 tablespoon at a time, until thoroughly incorporated. Pour the glaze over the cake and smooth evenly with a spatula. Let the cake sit 30 minutes before serving.

9. *To serve:* Cut into wedges and top each with a dollop of whipped cream.

BALINESE MANGO ICE CREAM WITH RUM

▪ CRAIG CLAIBORNE ▪

8 to 10 servings

2 fresh, ripe, unblemished mangoes
1 cup sugar
1 cup heavy cream
2 cups milk
5 large egg yolks
Salt
1 teaspoon vanilla extract
¼ cup dark rum

1. Cut the mango in half, discarding the seed. "Porcupine cut" each half, following *Truc #35*. Cut the flesh away from the outer peel.

2. Roughly chop the flesh and combine it in a mixing bowl with ½ cup of the sugar. Toss and then let it sit until the sugar dissolves, about 3 minutes.

3. In the top of a double boiler combine the cream, milk, egg yolks, remaining sugar, salt, and vanilla. Cook the custard, stirring continually so it does not stick to the pan.

4. Continue stirring until the custard is as thick as heavy cream and a candy thermometer reads 180°. Remove the custard from heat immediately, continuing to stir the mixture for 1 to 2 minutes more. Let the custard cool.

5. Add the mango mixture to the custard and blend. Stir in the rum.

6. Pour the mixture into the container of an ice-cream maker and freeze according to the manufacturer's instructions.

UPSIDE-DOWN PIE SHELL
▪ JIM DODGE ▪

One 9-inch crust

1 cup all-purpose flour
1½ teaspoons sugar
1 pinch salt
8 tablespoons (1 stick) unsalted butter
3 tablespoons heavy cream

SPECIAL UTENSILS:
2 metal 9-inch pie plates (see Truc #80*)*

1. Preheat the oven to 350°.
2. Combine the flour, sugar, and salt. Cut the butter into small pieces and blend with the flour until a coarse meal is formed.
3. Add the cream and carefully blend until the dough is smooth.
4. On a floured table, roll the dough into a 10-inch circle. Fold into quarters and unfold over one of the 9-inch pie plates. Trim the edges and place the other pie plate on top. Turn both plates upside down and bake on a sheet pan for 20 minutes. Turn over and remove the top pie plate. Continue baking until the bottom, center, and edge of the shell are golden. Set aside to cool.

DRY-POACHED PEARS WITH RED WINE SAUCE
▪ JIMMY SCHMIDT ▪

4 servings

Wine Sauce
1¼ cups red wine (preferably Pinot Noir)
1 cup sugar
3 tablespoons balsamic vinegar

Poached Pears
One 3-pound box kosher salt
4 large Comice pears
2 tablespoons unsalted butter
2 cups cinnamon ice cream
4 sprigs mint for garnish

1. *To make the wine sauce:* Bring the wine and sugar to a boil, reduce heat, and simmer until the wine reduces to 1 cup, about 20 minutes. Cool to room temperature and stir in vinegar. Set aside.
2. Preheat the oven to 450°.
3. Select a medium-size ovenproof pot, deep and wide enough to later accommodate all 4 pears. Fill the pot with the salt and heat in the oven for 60 minutes (see *Truc*

#36). Remove the pot and carefully pour out two-thirds of the salt and reserve. (Remember the salt is 450°!)

4. Insert a wooden skewer into each pear. Position the pears on top of the salt remaining in the pan. Don't let the pears touch each other. Pour the reserved hot salt back into the pan, burying the pears completely. Put the pan back into the oven and bake for 15 minutes, until tender.

5. Remove the pan from the oven and carefully pour out the salt. Brush away any clinging salt from the pears and set them on a platter to cool.

6. *To serve:* Spoon a puddle of wine sauce on the bottom of each plate. Put a pear in the middle of the sauce, add a scoop of ice cream on the side, and garnish with a mint sprig.

BARTLETT PEARS IN PUFF PASTRY
▪ JACQUES PÉPIN ▪

6 servings

1 cup flour—measured by dipping the cup directly into the flour and leveling it off with the hand
⅛ teaspoon salt
8 tablespoons unsalted butter, very cold (almost frozen), cut into 8 pieces
⅓ cup iced water
6 tablespoons sugar
¾ teaspoon ground cinnamon
Three 9-ounce ripe Bartlett pears
2 tablespoons freshly squeezed lemon juice (see Truc #31)
2 tablespoons unsalted butter at room temperature
⅓ cup water at room temperature
Heavy cream or sour cream, for garnish (optional)

1. Place the flour, salt and cold butter in a food processor and process for approximately 5 seconds. The butter should be lumpy and visible throughout the flour. Add the iced water and process another 4 to 5 seconds, just long enough for the mixture to become moist, even if it does not hold together completely and form a ball.

2. Transfer the contents to a lightly floured board, press together to form a compact ball, and roll into a rectangle about ¼ inch thick. Fold the ends of the rectangle until they meet in the center, then fold again to create a 4-layer dough. (This is called a *double turn*.) Immediately roll the dough again into a rectangle and fold it again into a double turn. Wrap in plastic wrap and refrigerate. The dough is now ready to use and can be prepared up to this point up to 1 day ahead.

3. Mix the sugar and cinnamon together and set aside. Peel the pears and cut in half lengthwise. Remove the core and seeds from each and arrange, cut side down, in one layer in a gratin dish. Sprinkle with the lemon juice and half the cinnamon-sugar mixture.

4. Preheat the oven to 375°.

5. Roll out the puff pastry (see *Truc #79*) and cut into 6 pieces, each about 5 × 3 inches. Lay a pastry piece on top of each pear and, as the pastry warms and relaxes slightly, press each piece gently around the pear so it takes on the shape of the pear half. Sprinkle with the remaining cinnamon-sugar mixture and dot with the butter.

6. Place the gratin dish on a cookie sheet and bake for about 25 minutes. The pastry should be browning nicely and the mixture around the pears should be bubbly and caramelized. Pour the water around the pears and return to the oven for 5 minutes. The water will melt the caramel and create a sauce. Eat lukewarm, with heavy cream or sour cream, if desired.

THE TRUCSTERS

We are grateful to these fine chefs—our trucsters—who welcomed us into their kitchens and showed us their trucs:

Lidia Bastianich, executive chef and co-owner of Felidia in New York City, author of *La Cucina di Lidia.*

Rick Bayless, executive chef and owner of Frontera Grill in Chicago, author of *Authentic Mexican.*

Rose Levy Beranbaum, author of *The Cake Bible* and *Rose's Christmas Cookies.*

David Bouley, executive chef and owner of Bouley, New York City.

Daniel Boulud, executive chef of Le Cirque in New York City.

Antoine Bouterin, executive chef of Le Perigord in New York City, author of *Cooking with Antoine at Le Perigord.*

Giuliano Bugialli, author of *Bugialli on Pasta,* and *The Fine Art of Italian Cooking, Foods of Italy,* and *Classic Techniques of Italian Cooking.*

David Burke, executive chef of the Park Avenue Café in New York City.

Yannick Cam, formerly of Le Pavillon in Washington, D.C., now executive chef of Yannick Cam at the Raddison Hotel in Alexandria, Virginia.

Craig Claiborne, former food editor for *The New York Times* and author of *The New York Times Cookbook, Craig Claiborne's Favorites,* and *A Feast Made for Laughter.*

Patrick Clark, formerly of Metro in New York City, now executive chef of Bice in Beverly Hills, California.

Eileen Crane, managing director and chief operating officer, Domaine Carneros by Taittinger, Carneros, California.

Andrew D'Amico, executive chef of Sign of the Dove in New York City.

Robert Del Grande, executive chef and co-owner of Cafe Annie in Houston.

Marcel Desaulniers, executive chef and owner of The Trellis in Williamsburg, Virginia, and author of *The Trellis Cookbook.*

Jean-Michel Diot, executive chef and co-owner of Park Bistro and Les Halles, New York City.

Jim Dodge, owner of American Baker in San Francisco and author of *Baking with Jim Dodge.*

Dean Fearing, executive chef of The Mansion on Turtle

Creek in Dallas and author of *Dean Fearing's Southwest Cuisine.*

Susan Feniger, chef and co-owner of City in Los Angeles and co-author of *City Cuisine.*

Michael Foley, executive chef and owner of Printer's Row in Chicago.

Larry Forgione, executive chef and owner of An American Place in New York City.

Hubert Keller, executive chef and co-owner of Fleur de Lys in San Francisco.

Emeril Lagasse, formerly of Commander's Palace, now executive chef and co-owner of Emeril's in New Orleans.

Pino Luongo, executive chef and co-owner of Le Madri in New York City and author of *A Tuscan in the Kitchen.*

Zarela Martinez, executive chef and owner of Zarela's in New York City.

Perla Meyers, author of *Perla Meyers' Art of Seasonal Cooking.*

Mary Sue Milliken, executive chef and co-owner of City in Los Angeles and co-author of *City Cuisine.*

Jean-Louis Palladin, executive chef and co-owner of Jean-Louis at the Watergate, Washington, D.C., and author of *Jean-Louis' Cooking with the Seasons.*

Charles Palmer, executive chef and co-owner of Aureole in New York City.

Gerard Pangaud, formerly of Aurora, now executive chef of The Ritz Carlton Hotel in Arlington, Virginia.

Jacques Pépin, chef and author of *The Short-Cut Cook, The Art of Cooking* (Vols. 1 and 2), *La Technique, La Methode,* and *Everyday Cooking with Jacques Pépin.*

Georges Perrier, executive chef and owner, Le Bec-Fin, Philadelphia.

Jacky Pluton, formerly of Le Truffe, Philadelphia, now executive chef at La Vieille Maison, Boca Raton, Florida.

Stephan Pyles, executive chef and co-owner of Routh Street Cafe in Dallas.

Jean-Jacques Rachou, executive chef and owner of La Côte Basque in New York City.

Leslee Reis, the late executive chef and owner of Café Provençal in Evanston, Illinois.

Michel Richard, executive chef and owner of Citrus in Los Angeles.

Michael Roberts, executive chef and co-owner of Trumps, Los Angeles, author of *Secret Ingredients.*

Judy Rogers, executive chef of Zuni Cafe in San Francisco.

Felipe Rojas-Lombardi, the late executive chef and co-owner of The Ballroom in New York City and author of *The Art of South American Cooking.*

Anne Rosenzweig, executive chef and co-owner of Arcadia in New York City and author of *The Arcadia Seasonal Mural and Cookbook.*

Alain Sailhac, dean of culinary studies, French Culinary Institute, New York City.

Jimmy Schmidt, executive chef and co-owner of The Rattlesnake Club in Detroit and author of *Cooking for All Seasons.*

André Soltner, executive chef and owner of Lutèce in New York City.

Jacques Torres, executive pastry chef of Le Cirque in New York City.

Barbara Tropp, executive chef and owner of China Moon Cafe in San Francisco and author of *The Modern Art of Chinese Cooking.*

Jean-Georges Vongerichten, executive chef and co-owner of JoJo in New York City and author of *Simple Cuisine.*

Jasper White, executive chef and co-owner of Jasper's in Boston and author of *Jasper White's Cooking from New England.*

Paula Wolfert, author of *Paula Wolfert's World of Food, Couscous and Other Good Food from Morocco,* and *The Cooking of Southwest France.*

INDEX

D

E